# America's Service Meltdown

# America's Service Meltdown

*Restoring Service Excellence in
the Age of the Customer*

Raul Pupo

 PRAEGER

AN IMPRINT OF ABC-CLIO, LLC
Santa Barbara, California • Denver, Colorado • Oxford, England

**Library of Congress Cataloging-in-Publication Data**

Pupo, Raul.
  America's service meltdown : restoring service excellence in the age of the customer / Raul Pupo.
    p. cm.
  Includes bibliographical references and index.
    ISBN 978-0-313-38602-2 (alk. paper) — ISBN 978-0-313-38603-9 (ebook)
1. Customer services—United States.   2. Customer relations—United States.   I. Title.
  HF5415.5.P87   2010
  658.8'12—dc22        2010006654

ISBN: 978-0-313-38602-2
EISBN: 978-0-313-38603-9

14   13   12   11   10      1   2   3   4   5

This book is also available on the World Wide Web as an eBook.
Visit www.abc-clio.com for details.

Praeger
An Imprint of ABC-CLIO, LLC

ABC-CLIO, LLC
130 Cremona Drive, P.O. Box 1911
Santa Barbara, California 93116-1911

This book is printed on acid-free paper (∞)

Manufactured in the United States of America

*A coeur vaillant rien d'impossible*

*Henry IV of France*

# Contents

# Preface

My views on service to the customer are largely the result of my training and years of experience running service businesses. I also believe that no less important in forging my views has been the role played by life experiences, some of which are very far from the world of business. If a discussion of these experiences can provide some insight into a further understanding of how best to serve a customer, then a brief biographical aside might be in order.

I was born in Havana, Cuba, and immigrated to New York City with my mother and father in the early 1950s. Despite President Fulgencio Batista's corrupt administration, with its clear ties to the U.S. Mafia, the reality of everyday life for apolitical Cubans was much different. In the 1950s, Cuba had a large middle class, and its workers enjoyed wages that on average exceeded those of workers in Belgium, Denmark, France, Japan, Australia, and Germany. (Other indicators proved that Cuba's "place in the sun" was more than just a geographic accident. For instance, per capita ownership of cars and televisions exceeded that of many European countries.[1] Infant mortality in 1957 was the lowest in Latin America and ahead of France, Belgium, Germany, Israel, Japan, Italy, Spain, and Portugal, and literacy was the third highest in Latin America.)[2]

Still, there was an undercurrent of serious civil discord. Not since 1902, when Cuba became a republic, has there been any significant period of time when political differences have been settled through the rule of law. My parents and I were simply our generation's members of a diaspora, which has existed throughout the island's history. Since Fidel Castro's arrival in 1959, of course, those prior human tragedies seem trivial by comparison.

The recollections I have as a child growing up in Cuba are experiences that were most often punctuated by the presence of a great deal of family cohesiveness and love in the home. Visits to see my mother's aunt, a woman of great warmth and finesse, who lived in a colonial-style house with a large period courtyard (a house eventually expropriated by Castro), and family outings to the blue-green waters of the beaches of Varadero on the northwest coast of the island and to my paternal grandmother's house—a house brimming with the sounds of children playing and laughing—proved to be profound and lasting lessons underscoring the value of family, love, friendship, and play.

Even as a child, however, I sensed that all wasn't right. Among family and friends, there was a near constant and excited chatter, oftentimes drifting into stage-whisper hushes, about how the latest assassinations, kidnappings, and bombings made clear the country was set to implode once again.

Against this backdrop, it is understandable that my parents had few qualms about leaving everything behind—their country, their relatives, and their home—such that their only son could have a normal future. In retrospect, their instinct about the future direction of the country was prophetic, and their decision to emigrate the only decision that could have been made under the circumstances. It is clear, too, with the benefit of more than 50 years of hindsight, that I stand as the clear beneficiary of my parents' courageous action.

My father worked as an accountant for a U.S.-based shipping company in Havana—his father, a promising tobacco planter in central Cuba, met an early death leaving behind a young widow and four small boys. He was terrific with numbers, and he drilled me constantly. (Actually, I could solve long-division problems the European way—with the vinculum upside down—long before I could string a coherent sentence together in English.) When my parents landed in New York, devoid as they were of professional or language skills, they had little choice but to take on whatever odd jobs came their way. My mother, most regrettably, ceased being a full-time mom and became instead a full-time laborer on the receiving dock of a Manhattan graphic arts printer.

From mom and dad, I learned the virtue of hard work, but as a latchkey child in a strange new land, I learned to survive strictly on instinct. I also developed discipline and self-reliance, qualities that I might not have honed as sharply as I did in a different setting. At the time, there were no church or civic programs available as there are today to ease the transition of new arrivals into the country. Worst of all was having to learn, in sink-or-swim fashion, a language that phonetically bore little resemblance to my native tongue. The Catholic grammar school my parents had chosen for me had a tough crowd, and as a consequence, the nuns ruled in a remarkably harsh fashion. The upshot was that life in school was only marginally better than life on the streets. Unbeknownst to my parents, and impudently for a 10-year-old, I rode the subway to make deliveries for a neighborhood florist to earn spending money.

When my parents grew increasingly frightened and weary of the difficult life in New York, we took a Greyhound bus and relocated to Miami. There, I attended public schools, worked after school making lamps for meager wages, and, discovering my interest in computers, began to read books on the subject in my spare time. My interest in computers was such that I even sat for a keypunch operator's test with the state of Florida. Though I passed the test with flying colors, I was subsequently informed that only women could work as keypunch operators for the state!

I attended college at the University of Miami. I have fond memories of my college years despite the fact that they unfolded during the worst bloodletting of the war in Vietnam. I took special pride, too, that no one had to drag me kicking and screaming to the local draft board. I went on my own out of a sense of duty to my adopted country. I'd be lying, of course, if I didn't admit to being equally happy that I was given a deferment that kept me from sloshing through rice paddies and being shot at. I never experimented with drugs—I find the word *experiment* to be a euphemism used by many who truly enjoyed doing drugs but who are afraid or embarrassed to admit it later in life—and so the only thing I have ever been tempted to inhale is the smoke of a good Cuban cigar.

Somehow, while I was at the University of Miami, I found time to start a delivery service—the Rocket Express! The delivery business started with $500, all of it borrowed, succeeded despite my inexperience and the presence of entrenched, well-capitalized competitors. How did we do it? The implication for me is clear. Our microbusiness had absolutely no tangible advantage over the others. We simply had to think differently. And, by putting the customer's interest and welfare above all else, we pushed the boundaries of conventional thinking. We, in essence, ran the business around the proposition that *customers are first*. Our customers told us that other suppliers simply had too many rules that got in the way of effectively serving their end-customers. Other delivery companies would not guarantee pickup times, drop-off times, or the number of stops in a day. Some would handle only certain kinds of merchandise, and still others would not agree to climb stairs to gather the merchandise. Well, the Rocket Express had absolutely no problem agreeing to these requirements. Our business grew nicely from nothing. The competition had no idea what hit them. They simply were ossified by their own procedures. I was to repeat this formulation, in an entirely different business context, successfully time and time again. Eventually, my father took over and ran the business as I entered the computer field.

My first computer-related job involved managing a four-person data-processing department for the aluminum products division of a building materials company. In addition to overseeing the operations of the department, I also wrote programs in FORTRAN that helped schedule plant production and track inventory. Our division was located in Miami, while the mainframe computer was in Tampa, Florida. As a result, every so often I would hop on an airplane, or drive, with a box full of punched cards so that I could run our data and programs through the corporate computer and return with output reports. Later we were able to make a quantum leap and enter the telecommunications age by transmitting information via punched paper tape. A model of efficiency it was not, as it took two people to transmit a spool of paper tape: one person threaded the tape through the reader and kept it from twisting; the other would insert a pencil through the spool, and while holding the pencil with two hands, allow the spool to unwind while it was being read! Still, users unaware of the process we went through to "make sausage" seemed pleased that accurate inventory and cost data was available when needed.

After I received my undergraduate degree, I was hired by Eastman Kodak in Rochester, New York. The work at Kodak involved designing automated systems to speed the flow of equipment orders through the company's huge and aging distribution system. Kodak, for a corporation of its size and very much set in its ways after being in business nearly 100 years, had an unusually keen awareness of the need to serve the customer—its dealer network. It was a rickety infrastructure, however, that continually got in the way of satisfying its service mission. (In chapter 4 we will talk about the role that a business process infrastructure plays in satisfying a service mission.)

While I worked at Kodak, I took an MBA degree in information systems from the Rochester Institute of Technology (RIT). RIT's cross-town rival, the University of Rochester, where I had initially enrolled, steadfastly refused to allow me to take a full academic load while I also worked full time. I pleaded with the dean that if my grades weren't up to par, I would agree to reduce my load. No dice. Policy was policy. I was not a very happy customer, and so, after my first semester at the university, I did the only sensible thing to do: I voted with my feet and enrolled at RIT, where they were only too happy to oblige so long as my grades didn't suffer and the tuition was paid. The school, as it turned out, was my kind of place, as the courses were taught mostly by practitioners.

Armed with my MBA, I went to work for Big Eight accounting firm Touche Ross & Co. as a computer consultant. There, all young staffers toiled with a singular focus to rack up billable hours for the firm. Still, the experience and skills learned proved to be of great benefit. After I left Touche Ross, I went to work for a division of Evans Products Company, a building materials company with $1.2 billion in sales. After eight-plus years in charge of the division's computer system activities, and being in the running to head one of the company's regional profit centers, my career came to a screeching halt courtesy of corporate raider Mr. Victor Posner.

Seizing on the company's low valuation, Posner began taking a position in Evans stock in 1980 through his investment vehicle, Sharon Steel Corporation, a company he had raided years earlier and that he now controlled. The jamboree was in full swing, however, beginning in April 1983, when he installed his children and cronies on the Evans board, sacked division presidents and other key executives, moved company headquarters to his North Miami Beach condominium, and proceeded to dismantle the company. Having exhausted all of his options to save the company by selling or spinning off divisions or merging the company into Sharon Steel—a move blocked by Sharon Steel's lenders—Mr. Posner had no choice but to force Evans into bankruptcy in 1985. That same year, Mr. Posner earned in excess of $23 million and was far and away America's highest paid executive![3]

Mr. Posner eventually got his comeuppance—he pleaded no contest to tax evasion and fraud and was slapped with a $6 million fine; he was barred by the SEC from participating in the management of a public company for life; and he was even sued by his son—but not before his depredations crushed whatever stockholder value was left of Evans and, most regrettably, disrupted if not destroyed the lives of many working families.

I was to suffer a double setback. In addition to having my career abort just when it seemed I was hitting my stride, I was forced to relocate from the city of Philadelphia to find a new job before I could complete the final requirement—writing and presenting a research thesis—for a master of science degree in technology management from the University of Pennsylvania. After Mr. Posner, it was time to start over again. And, so I did. I was to spend the next 28 years starting and running information technology service businesses.

My motivation to write this book comes after a long gestation and after my having decided that although I believe many service concepts are intuitive, common sense, and come to some individuals innately (the inclination to *serve* is probably deeply buried in character, which might explain why some people get it while others don't), many have to be studied, learned, and applied.

In this book, we will not nibble at the margins. There is too much of that in print, and most of it never gets to the heart of why large companies and small dish out manifestly poor service to customers on a regular basis. The reader will find that we deal with matters of substance and leave pronouncements to "smile and look the customer in the eye" for others to make.

# Introduction

The most powerful nation on the face of the earth is seeing its businesses experience nothing less than a *service meltdown*. This is the case despite decades of jawboning by executives of both large and small American companies about the importance of customer service excellence. Each time a consultant or academic publishes a work lauding an organization for its world-class service practices, they prove my point by citing the exception. To be sure, the problem of poor customer service is not confined to the United States. According to a worldwide customer satisfaction survey conducted in 2007 by consulting giant Accenture, 59 percent of consumers quit doing business with suppliers for reasons having to do with poor service. Worse, the survey goes on to report, 41 percent of global respondents describe service quality as fair, poor, or terrible, and only 5 percent describe it as excellent.[1] This *service deficit* (I prefer the term *deficit* to *gap* as it speaks not just to a quality that is lacking but one that is also *wanting*) afflicts all industries, with the health care sector usually bringing up the rear.[2]

The disappointment is that the United States, despite its economic prowess and uniqueness among major nations in having come out of the carnage of World War II largely unscathed, has been unable to take advantage of its head start to become the unquestioned champion of service in the world. Consumers who yearn for the good old days when nattily clad gas station attendants would pump gasoline in their cars and put air in their tires as emblematic of service need to be reminded that for a large portion of the population, "separate but equal" public accommodations in restaurants, motels, stores, beaches, and parks hardly frames a nostalgic and positive reference of *service*.

The bemusement, for me, has been to witness the continuing failure of many in business to have a solid grasp of the meaning of *service*. If we recall that *service* means work that is done for or on behalf of others, how is it that we so often do what is in *our* self-interest rather than what is in the best interest of those we are presumably trying to serve? The inescapable answer has to be that service, consciously or not, is somehow seen as a necessary evil in the normal conduct of business. In the service and information age, exploiting the fundamental weakness of this conventional wisdom uniquely benefits the customer-focused provider.

What do I say in this book about service to the customer that has not been said before? The answer is in two parts. First, while it is true that service as an important management topic has resulted in a prodigious volume of books, articles, and seminars, few, if any, of these sources make reference to what should properly be called the *critical success factors* in service. These are the factors that trace a straight line from service to the customer to the success of the firm. What I have done in this book is to draw an imaginary arc below which is found a seemingly endless list of nostrums that incrementally adds little or no value to the customer—and consequently to the service provider. We will spend little or no time discussing these as they amount to nothing more than so much window dressing. Above the arc is where the action is: 80 percent of the resources, energy, and focus available to the enterprise must be directed to the factors above the arc. Second, every function in the organization has the potential—a potential which must be actively sought and exploited—to impact service delivery as perceived or in fact. A failure to act on this interrelatedness ensures that service actions remain disconnected and ad hoc, the domain of the poor souls pigeonholed in the customer service department whose one job it is to deal with pesky customers.

The critical success factors must work holistically—as a system—for excellent service to result. Leave any of these elements out and you suck out the oxygen needed to contribute to the growth and vitality of the customer-focused enterprise. In this book you will read about a pursuit of service excellence that focuses on these factors.

What are the critical success factors required of excellence in service?

1. *Leadership from the top*—Business leaders grant that service is an important road map to success. Pronouncements to that

effect fill the halls of corporate America. Yet, consumers continue to vote with their feet as they seek alternate suppliers. What's going on? The key issue—that which catalyzes all other critical success factors—is leadership. The customer-focused organization demands a special kind of leadership. A leader whose calling card is that he is charismatic, politically adroit, and well spoken won't cut it. The epic battles that are sure to ensue to transform today's organization into a customer-focused service provider will melt the resolve of most leaders. The customer-focused leader must have the moral courage to challenge long-held assumptions, make tough decisions, implement needed reforms, and, in the end, raise what is intellectually sound to an emotional level. In the absence of this kind of commitment from senior-most management, service will continue as nothing more than an afterthought, something to deal with only in the face of serious customer discontent. Further, a customer-focused leader needs to set ego aside, yet remain a confident leader—*confident* meaning that he is comfortable, that is to say, not threatened, and that he seeks, supports, and gives wide berth to other leaders throughout the organization in their mission to serve the customer. That brand of leadership, I find, is a scarce commodity.

2. *The customer as the centerpiece of strategy*—Service to the customer as a meaningful business strategy is bankrupt. Classic business strategy formulation has companies think long and hard about their strengths and weaknesses before organizing around a given competitive strategy. Some companies focus on leveraging unique corporate resources, such as patents and copyrights, in specialty markets; others may channel their efforts on achieving cost leadership; and still others may choose to differentiate their products or services on the basis of superior technology or brand image. In the end, the selected strategy gives direction to a long-term vision, a mission statement, financial goals, organizational structures, technology initiatives, and so on. The process is rigorous, formal, and analytical. The role of the customer, however, is hardly explicit in most of what we understand to be the process of strategy formulation. Harvard University professor Michael Porter is the father of a company's need to organize around one of the aforementioned generic

strategies. But scan the index—or better yet, read the whole book—of his seminal work, *Competitive Strategy,* and you will not find one single entry on *customer service,* or *service* for that matter![3]

A customer-focused organization, on the other hand, *centers* its business strategy around the customer. The consequential differences in the two approaches are striking: Can anyone in his right mind imagine a customer demanding of his lender a mortgage whose principal balance increases based on the lowest monthly payment option? Incredibly, Wachovia Bank's Pick-A-Pay mortgage was just such a product before the business imploded! We'll have more to say about Wachovia's misdeeds in chapter 1.

3. *A service ethic*—The organization that is genuine about its commitment to the customer needs to actively promote and enforce an ethical standard that, above all else, celebrates and rewards employees for satisfying customer needs and for always acting with integrity. Lapses in integrity erode trust, and this, in turn, erects barriers to the free exchange of candid information so vital to the pursuit of excellence in service. A service ethic can only thrive in an environment of hard-hitting, frank, and open discussion both inside and outside the enterprise. High integrity is necessary not just to rid the organization of obviously wrongful and dishonest acts, but also to preclude more insidious forms of ethical misbehavior: an organization that knowingly overcommits, overpromises, or oversells can suffer ethical lapses potentially more injurious to its relationship with customers than any process malfunction.

The subprime mortgage crisis of 2007, which resulted in numerous bank failures and cost millions of Americans their homes and hundreds of thousands their jobs, is one case in point. Another is the monstrous Ponzi scheme pulled off by former NASDAQ stock exchange chairman Bernard Madoff, which will cost clients of his investment firm—many of whom were friends and family—more than $65 billion. These are but two examples of the volatile cocktail that results when organizations ignore the service ethic in favor of a casino culture with greed and corruption mixed in for good measure. The service ethic, of all the critical success factors, has proved the most elusive for businesses to grasp.

4. *Power to the front line*—Human capital, intelligent, skilled, and properly supported and equipped, is the fundamental resource that adds value to the customer-focused organization. My definition of a frontline worker is, therefore, correspondingly broad: anyone who has regular contact with the customer is by my definition on the front line. This includes sales executives, nurses, call-center personnel, flight attendants, and bank tellers. Clearly, this definition challenges the conventional wisdom and image of a frontline worker as a low-paid individual of modest skills on the fringe of the organization. This view is no longer workable, and a broader perspective on this important organizational role is inevitable. Two other things have to change: (1) the skill sets necessary to effectively interact with the customer—a complex of upgraded attributes and abilities is now called for as never before—and (2) the organization's support of, investment in, and empowerment of human resources on the front line. The need for these changes, as we will discuss, should sound an alarm to senior executives who seek quick-fix solutions: service at the front, the mechanics of which are just as much art as they are science, pivots on the competence, preparation, support, and dedication of individuals distant from the executive suite.

The absolutely decisive factor of production today, says Peter Drucker, in his book *The Post Capitalist Society*, is knowledge. And, knowledge, more and more, is found not in bosses but in workers.[4] Frontline people by the very nature of their work and proximity to the customer have the potential to become the knowledge workers par excellence of the enterprise in the service and information age. This potential, however, remains largely unfulfilled to the detriment of both businesses and customers alike.

A full expression of service to the customer can only be found in an environment where these critical success factors—a committed leadership, a customer-centric business strategy, a compatible culture, and a competent organization—work in harmony. No one critical success factor, working in isolation, can be the determining factor, regardless of how much corporate might is put behind it. The interplay of the four factors is complex and interrelated. The most competent frontline organization money can buy, for example, operating without effective tools or led by a lackadaisical management team will have little if any effect on the service performance of the organization.

Each of the four critical success factors commands a chapter in the book. We conclude the book with a final chapter that takes on some of the most hotly debated service-related topics in business today. How does service impact profitability? How does the organization gauge service to the customer? How does customer satisfaction differ from customer loyalty? How does customer acquisition relate to customer retention? What is the principal motivation behind outsourcing? We'll provide answers to these and other topical questions in ways that will almost always seem unexpected, largely because they cut against the grain of current orthodoxy. I believe that although service remains firmly anchored to the enterprise in economic terms, a number of economic misconceptions about the nature of service persist, which continue to dog its aggressive pursuit. These we try to set straight.

Most of what I have to say in this book is based on my experience founding, building, leading, and advising business-to-business technology service companies. That the businesses I have led—all started with modest amounts of capital—operated successfully and had lucrative exits in the fiercely competitive information technology industry is a testament to the power that can be harnessed by the *lever of service*. In finance, debt can supplement equity to leverage or increase purchasing power. In physics, leverage can be used to mechanical advantage, or as Archimedes, the greatest mathematician of antiquity, famously said, "Give me a place to stand and I shall move the Earth." In the service and information age, *service* must be added to the list of classical *factors of production*—land, labor, and capital—and exploited to its fullest. No other factor of production will yield equivalent leverage.

I believe that the lessons espoused in this book are universal. It doesn't matter whether you are bootstrapping a start-up enterprise—where poor service practices have less of a chance to hide behind deep pockets—or managing a far-flung corporation—where an entrepreneurial spirit may have long flickered out. It doesn't matter if you are in the manufacture of hard goods or in a service business, if your business is foreign or domestic, or if you are operating in a bricks-and-mortar realm or electronically. The principles and practices discussed herein run a common thread through any business—and indeed through nonprofit sectors such as government and education where there seems to be gathering a growing sense of service awareness.

I am not a theorist. I am a practitioner, an entrepreneur. I have lived and championed the principles and practices we will discuss in this book every day for more than 30 years, and I can attest to their superior power in cementing customer relationships for the long term.

Yes, businesses abound that are *not* customer focused. And, yes, many have been financially successful over stretches of time—maybe even long stretches. In the service and information age, however, ignoring the customer for long is a sure bet that executives will spend more time managing churn than managing the business. It gets worse. Ignoring the customer tempts the enterprise to cut corners, often resulting in the severest of consequences. We will discuss some of these in this book. To my way of thinking, the principles and practices discussed in this book prove to be, in the end, a morally superior business ideal—doing as promised, in business as in life, is always a morally superior standard.

My goal in this book is to examine these principles and practices so as to challenge the reader to question both his approach and that of his organization's to service. The heavy lifting, of course, will have to be done by executive leaders who may or may not have the stomach for the battle that, of necessity, must be joined in order to replace obsolete service practices with a fresh and dynamic approach to serving the customer. It is not inappropriate, given the many challenges ahead, to be reminded of the motto first used by the elite Special Air Service (SAS) regiment of the British army, which cut its teeth behind the lines of Rommel's Nazi army in North Africa: "Who dares wins."

# Leadership from the Top

Leadership is a process of morality to the degree that leaders engage with followers on the basis of shared motives and values and goals.

—*James Mcgregor Burns*
*Leadership*

Having traveled on business for the better part of four decades, I have frequent-flier accounts with all the major airlines. With all the mileage credits I have accumulated over the years, an upgrade to first class should be the rule and not the exception. When I asked for an upgrade on a recent United Airlines flight, the agent told me, "We are completely booked; no seat is available in the first class cabin." Upon boarding the jet, I realized that first class was full because a flight crew was occupying more that half the seats! How could they deny a privilege to a prized customer while seating their own employees in first class? I asked a flight attendant, "Why don't you allow your customers with upgrades to have priority seating in first class? The answer, clearly missing the point of my question, left me light headed: "Sir," the flight attendant said, "we have a union agreement that allows a crew 'dead-heading' back to their home base the privilege of flying in the first class cabin. Sorry."

When the executives from United Airlines sat across the negotiating table from the union, they didn't realize that compromises, made at the expense of the customer, constitute bad trade-offs for the organization. Yet, some executive should have thought of that since this is an employee-owned airline. Management actions like these are more convincing than any number of slogans to the contrary. Namely, the customer does *not* come first with this airline!

If a company's executive leadership fails to adopt a customer-focused strategy, others in the organization get the message. Absent any kind of heroic actions on behalf of customers by frontline employees acting on their own, the customer loses because the leaders through their behavior set the tone for apathetic service behavior. Gradually, customer satisfaction begins to fade. And if slipshod service behavior is left unattended, customer attrition sets in as customers identify substitute providers.

In their book *The Real Heroes of Business,* authors Len Schlesinger and Bill Fromm profile 14 service workers—waitress, salesman, hotel doorman, and others—from diverse industries. The accounts are vivid and indeed represent some of the best-of-the-best frontline work anywhere. It is emblematic of the inability of executive leadership to institutionalize service behavior in the enterprise, however, that by the authors' reckoning, these service workers have had to figure out how to deliver excellent service *on their own* (italics mine).[1] That the subtitle of the book is *And Not a CEO among Them,* underscores the persistent vacuum of service leadership in today's enterprise.

## LEADERSHIP IN THE SERVICE AND INFORMATION AGE

Service leadership, or customer-focused leadership, is my characterization of a leadership style that gives life, through its actions, to an organization's customer focus. Successful service leadership cannot be produced by the blind mirroring of the norms established for the leadership of the industrial age. I believe most executives today understand that new market forces have changed the economic landscape in dramatic ways. I also believe, however, that few executives grasp the consequent impact of these economic changes on their own leadership actions and by extension on their organizations' service behavior. This disconnect, in my view, has rendered many companies *institutionally incapable*—incapable organizationally, behaviorally, culturally—of delivering excellence in service to the customer as leadership models of old remain entrenched. To be blunt, these companies have made a *habit* of rendering mediocre service. As with most habits, this pattern of behavior will be hard to break. Unfortunately, these organizations might already have fallen too far behind to realistically entertain the prospect of challenging the service leaders in their peer industry group.

The fundamentals of the industrial age are very different from those of the service and information age. The industrial age emphasized regimented labor and swift capital formation for investment in plant, property, and equipment as the primary factors of production; bulk mattered. Industrial-age models of economic behavior focus on efficiency, short-term thinking, uniformity, and mass production. Conversely, human potential, creativity, and information are the primary resource strengths of the service-and-information-age enterprise. These two views offer a graphic contrast of the deep business philosophical and cultural divide that has been with us for some time and that will take effective leadership to eventually bridge.

When I was a young computer consultant working for Big Eight accounting firm Touche Ross & Co., the singular focus was on client-billable hours. Few things mattered more to the firm, and it set off fierce competition among staff to be among the leaders in billable hours. Kudos and bonuses—more of the former and less of the latter if you were a young staff member—came your way in direct proportion to your billable hours. In later years, I was to fire the consultants of accounting firm Arthur Andersen on two different occasions—I guess I didn't learn my lesson the first time!—for running the meter on our company. Andersen's demise in 2002, not unexpectedly, came at the expense of the public's interest—that is, the customer's interest—as it pursued a culture that demanded ever-increasing levels of billable fees no matter what.[2]

In the industrial age, workers were understood to be fungible. Corporate strategy, such as it was, focused on efficiency of production. The principal tool of strategy thus became the learning curve—factories could reasonably be expected to drop their unit cost predictably with each doubling of production volume. In service work, adherence to this model is assuredly counterproductive. One of the largest Internet service providers in the nation, for example, requires its call-center teams to meet a quota of numbers of customers served each hour or risk losing their incentive bonus. Not only does this approach fly in the face of the need to devolve power to the front line for effective customer service, but it also fails to recognize that production incentives and quotas—in lieu of a practice that ensures that customers have all of their questions answered without a quick brush-off—are vestiges of a time long past.

Even U.S. military doctrine, to this day, is a vestige of our industrial past, reliant as it is on industrial and logistical strength, overwhelming force, and power on power—qualities that have been rendered obsolete by the small wars of the 21st century. Service-and-information-age models, both in commerce as in the military, stress effectiveness, knowledge, access to information, high-speed communications, and small, tailored volumes of production.

## BUGGY-WHIP ACCOUNTING IS OBSOLETE

Leadership in the service and information age calls for senior executives to break loose of the stranglehold of industrial-age accounting. Virtually all of the accounting practices we know today are vintage World War I. These practices were developed by managers seeking to grasp the cost implications of the complex economic activity that began to take place within the new vertically integrated industrial enterprises of the time. For the most part, these practices proved to be very successful in providing managers the information needed to measure and control *operational* activity within their enterprises.

Those same practices, however, designed though they were to track internal plant efficiencies, eventually became the principal means of providing financial information for external reporting purposes. The then-emerging capital markets, especially, became a driving force for financial reports, which could subsequently be audited by independent accountants. How it came to be that these industrial-age financial *reporting* practices, with little or no changes in the intervening 90 years, became widely adopted by executives to *run* their enterprises and by outsiders to gauge the worth of those enterprises is not entirely clear. Regardless, these practices, if they were not irrelevant then are clearly so today. Here are some of the principal reasons why this is so:

1. **Industrial-age accounting has no reliable metrics for valuing intellectual capital such as people, processes, relationships, and ideas.** Revenue, labor, and expense transactions can be counted by accountants without breaking a sweat. Now ask these same professionals how to value a customer relationship, a channel partner alliance, a service initiative, an innovation, an idea, or a brand, and they draw a blank. In the service and information age, the focus needs to be on

valuing the quality of the management team, the company's business model, its customer relationships, its service processes, and its intellectual property—patents, copyrights, trademarks, and trade secrets. None of these assets are anywhere to be found on a company's balance sheet.

It is clear, therefore, that a stubborn insistence on information gleaned strictly from financial statements will almost always yield an erroneous conclusion regarding the franchise value of firms whose principal assets are intangible. Granted, valuation experts can determine an appraisal value for a *given* intangible asset. The process, however, is arduous and expensive. Moreover, because the appraisal method requires dart throws to arrive at a pro forma of financial performance for the asset in question—the younger the asset the more darts that have to be flung—the resultant valuation is uniquely subjective.

2. **Financial measures tell the story of events already completed.** Industrial-age financial measures have no predictive value whatsoever. These methods were developed for the purpose of accounting for historical transactions, not predicting them. Equity accounting is indeed a retrospective view of where the enterprise has been, not where it is going. This look into the rearview mirror, arguably adequate for smokestack companies, can hardly be effective in its ability to forecast the direction and velocity of enterprises in the Internet age.

3. **Industrial-age financial reporting exaggerates the short term.** Outlays for improved processes, service initiatives, brand development, and frontline education are considered period expenses under conventional accounting rules, potentially depressing short-term financial results. What is the best way to improve the firm's short-term profit picture? Mortgage the future by throttling outlays in the current period.

In classical economics, it is understood that not everything of value has a price. That might explain why the professionals have such a hard time valuing firms born of the service and information age. Physical assets—property, plant, and equipment—and even money are now commoditized. These tangible assets are playing a waning role in the success of the firm in the service and information age. Enterprise success today is based fundamentally on the quality of people and their potential to build intellectual capital.

There is more. At present, only 14 percent of the workforce in the nation is engaged in the physical transformation or production of goods, the vast majority of the workforce being engaged in service-related labor. The number of workers in commodity-producing industries has been steadily declining for decades and is expected to continue its decline. Even firms engaged in the production of goods are seeing an increase in the ratio of service to production labor cost. It will be a rare firm, therefore, that will not see its cost of sales dominated by service activities.

This turn of events poses little problem for industrial-age accounting practices. Industrial-age accounting can effectively track labor expenses traceable to a unit of production. More and more, however, the modern enterprise finds that before it can deliver services of even moderate complexity to the customer, it must engage in interactions, inside and outside the firm, in order that it can *be* in a position to effectively deliver such services. *Service interactions* are more than just another indirect labor overhead item; these interactions actually represent an intangible asset of the firm. Interactions that can include identifying, qualifying, analyzing, negotiating, pricing, coordinating, integrating, monitoring, and reporting are all part of a complex web of service activities required by the firm to remain competitive in a constantly changing marketplace. Properly conducted and swiftly executed, these interactions can add value to the firm in very real ways.

Service interactions with all of their complexity, ambiguity, and fuzziness will permeate the firm without regard to hierarchical, departmental, functional, or product boundaries. As this comes to pass, no amount of financial wizardry will enable industrial-age models of accounting and finance, designed as they were to follow product through the plant, to faithfully represent the value and worth of the firm in the new century.

In the end, the actual value of an asset—tangible or intangible— is what someone is willing to pay for it. This probably explains how it is that the stock market *indirectly* values a company's intangible assets to an extent that the accounting profession struggles mightily to achieve using more direct methods of valuation. As I write this account, the price-to-book ratio of companies such as SAP is 6.88; Apple, 8.12; and Amazon, 20.01. This ratio compares a company's market valuation to the value of its hard assets as indicated on its balance sheet. SAP's price-to-book ratio indicates that only 15 percent (1/6.88) of its value is made up of hard assets, and that, therefore, 85 percent of the value of the company is accounted for by intangibles. Similarly, Apple's intangibles add up to 87 percent, and Amazon's to 95 percent. This trend, toward diminished hard asset values relative to intangible assets, is inexorable and is likely to embrace companies in every business sector of the economy.

## INDUSTRIAL-AGE MYOPIA IS NOT DEAD BY A LONG SHOT

For some time now, we have been a witness to the collision of industrial-age views of enterprise management with those of the service and information age. Few doubt that the former will eventually falter. But, make no mistake about it, industrial-age views are prevalent now and will, for some time to come, continue to dominate the thinking and actions of individuals in virtually every business sector. I have been a participant in many spirited boardroom debates dealing with everything from service company valuations to the expenditure of funds for service initiatives to the justification of payrolls for service management executives, and much more— enough to know that there is still a great deal of industrial-age Kool-Aid to go around. An executive who takes a long-term view, especially if such a view runs the risk of impinging on short-term financial objectives, will not be endeared to industrial-age constituencies and thus will have to fight for every inch of ground.

Constituencies that include boards of directors, institutional shareholders, investment bankers, research analysts, and accountants all seem to have a genetic disinclination to take the long view, which is required to allow the customer-focused provider to establish solid relationships in the marketplace. These constituencies are all a product of the same financial ethos that demands hard, easy-to-measure, financial results *now*. Enterprise executives, for their part, know on which side their bread is buttered: short-term financial objectives are just fine so long as executive short-term incentives and bonuses are in keeping with such goals!

Frederick Reichheld, in his book *The Loyalty Effect*, agrees. Reichheld says that "the tendency to regard short-term profit as the primary business objective has become more and more pronounced in both business schools and boardrooms."[3] The customer-focused provider with the core of its strategy resting on people, processes, and other intangible assets needs to free itself from the claustrophobic grip of short-term financial measures if it is to make its service vision a reality. This all takes time, but it must begin with executive leaders as change agents.

Effective and courageous leadership is needed to counteract—*counterattack* is a better word—the obsession with short-term performance metrics and hard-asset accounting yardsticks in the face of the challenges of the service and information age. I believe these measures as *exclusive* metrics of enterprise value and performance should be relegated to the archaeological dustbin of the industrial age. Until such time, however, the full value of the intangibles of the enterprise, as the driving force behind a business strategy based on service, will never take hold. If there is an elephant in the room that keeps firms from rendering excellence in service, I believe it is the industrial-age fixation with financial performance.

## WHAT TO LOOK FOR IN A CUSTOMER-FOCUSED LEADER

The top-most leadership in an enterprise—a group that obviously counts the CEO but which can include the company's COO, EVP, divisional general managers, managing directors, and so on—can and does have the most to say about whether the company adopts a customer-focused culture. And, whether the executive arrives at his beliefs in a customer focus instinctively or through experience—or both—*conviction* in the practice of serving the customer as the overarching objective of the enterprise is a must. The alternative to a leadership without this strongly held conviction will be yet another enterprise that offers more lip service than customer service. Other characteristics, as we will point out, must also be present in the senior leadership as these are similarly fundamental to the success of the customer-focused provider. (In this discussion, I'm assuming the executive brings the requisite industry, functional, and technical know-how to the position.)

Here are some of the more important attributes of the customer-focused leader:

- *Personal.* Executives must have integrity first and foremost. They must be honest; they must do as promised. They must be trustworthy. They must live what they preach. They must possess moral courage to withstand, at times, fierce opposition.
- *Interpersonal.* Few attributes are more important than the ability to listen; to be open-minded at all times. Executives must be effective communicators with the ability to tone their message according to their audience.

- *Motivational.* Executives must exhibit a passion for their customer-focused culture; they must exhort their workers to perform as advertised. They must be self-confident, self-motivated, and decisive. They must also be inspirational.
- *Leadership style.* A customer focus requires rapid adaptability and flexibility on the part of executives. Executives must be comfortable dealing in grey areas; they must see the forest from the trees. They must be empathetic and positive in outlook; they must lead as much with their hearts as with their minds.

Senior leaders must exhibit great tenacity of purpose in their mission. Strategic change can be a long and arduous journey, and leaders are certain to be challenged each and every step of the way. Believe me, a leader who is tasked with transforming his organization will at times feel he is trapped deep behind enemy lines. As Niccolò Machiavelli advises aspiring and valorous new princes, ". . . there is nothing more difficult to take in hand, more perilous to conduct, or more uncertain in its success, than to take the lead in the introduction of a new order of things."[4] The ability to stay the course will serve leaders well when the more expedient thing to do would be to kowtow to industrial-age constituencies. Again, Machiavelli is instructive as he points out that "the innovator has for enemies all those who have done well under the old conditions, and lukewarm defenders in those who may do well under the new."[5] Strong leadership is therefore necessary because although the direction of an organization's march toward a customer focus may be clear in the executive's mind, its exact route can never be known before setting out on the journey.

Finally, I have worked with many customer-focused executives who were very effective in their leadership roles. Few, it is fair to say, had heroic qualities: great charisma, towering personalities, or unusual creativity. They were not celebrity executives, and they certainly did not walk on water. They all possessed one thing, however: an unwavering conviction to uphold a mission of service to the customer. *That* is the kind of executive leadership we should all wish to be surrounded by in the service and information age.

### WHERE TO FIND A CUSTOMER-FOCUSED LEADER?

Person for person, small entrepreneurial service companies are more often led by service-savvy leaders than are large enterprises.

Individuals with strong service leadership skills are generally attracted to the young and growing firm where attitudes, habits, and opinions on service have not yet been hardened into ineffectiveness by the onset of bureaucracy. For that reason, small entrepreneurial firms have always been my preferred source of customer-focused executives. As a rule, however, I know of no wellspring of compatible executive characteristics from which to tap. Certainly, as a nation, we haven't the pool of executive talent that could rival, say, the source of executives steeped in marketing, finance, or engineering. The reason, of course, is that we just don't have a history, a legacy, of excelling in service. Meanwhile, postsecondary education in the fundamental principles and practices of how the enterprise should serve the customer remains almost universally anemic and is in need of major reform.

My graduate school alma mater, the Rochester Institute of Technology, is a case in point. The university has done more in this area than most institutions of higher learning by offering an MS degree in service leadership and innovation. The degree requirements of 48 quarter credit hours, however, include a core of only 20 quarter credit hours—five courses—on service management. Worse, as I scan the course catalog, I'm not sure I can find more than three courses that deal with the subject matter in a substantive way!

A company that is seriously committed to a culture of service is probably best served by doing as I have had to do for many years in the light of the general paucity that exists of service-savvy executives: train and groom your own cadre of executive talent. I believe that executives can be taught to behave in ways consistent with a customer-focused attitude. I am also a big believer, however, in the nature argument of leadership, which holds that leaders are largely born. One quick look at the list of attributes I enumerated above should lead the reader to conclude that those attributes are either innate or not in the individual. If they are not, there is no number of rock-climbing retreats the executive team can repair to that will develop those individuals into effective leaders. Any executive development program, therefore, needs to start with a pool of executive talent whose skill potential can blossom through training and experience.

## WHAT CUSTOMER-FOCUSED LEADERS MUST DO

In this book, I stress those critical success factors required of the enterprise to render excellence in service. The first—the agent provocateur—of these factors is executive leadership, not executive *management* but executive *leadership*. Management stresses doing things right, leadership is all about doing the right things. What are the key roles of the executive in the customer-focused organization?

1. **Leaders must believe they are in business to *serve* customers.** In an incredibly telling survey, Walker Information, a research firm, conducted a telephone interview among 121 companies from among the *Forbes* 500 to determine the extent of their customer focus. In that survey, only 44 percent of the executive respondents strongly agreed with the assertion that their company exists primarily to service customers.[6] If that doesn't strike you as a profound failure to grasp the reason for a business to *be* in business, then nothing will.

   Believing you are in business to serve customers means ensuring that the company's strategy and plans are framed around *customers*, not markets, products, or technologies. Executives must ensure that the customer remains the centerpiece of any final go-to-market strategy as this will give direction to downstream operational plans. Companies such as Digital Equipment Corporation (DEC), Wang Laboratories, and Polaroid, darlings of Wall Street for a time, all forgot this rather fundamental lesson as they became enamored of their own products. In the end, these once mighty companies all left the scene.

   My experience with DEC and its founder, Ken Olsen, is particularly instructive in this connection. The last time I met Mr. Olsen was at Boston's Museum of Fine Arts. The museum was having a Monet exhibition, and we were guests of Mr. Olsen's company. Our company was a devotee of DEC's then high-flying VAX series of minicomputers—a category of computer largely invented by DEC. Our beef with the company was that we could get no attention from the sales and service organization. I mean zero! I said as much to Mr. Olsen when I met him. He replied rather dismissively, "DEC is a computer company. We want to make the best computer in the industry." Predictably, Mr. Olsen lost his grip on the company shortly thereafter. Eventually, the company became a part of Compaq, which in turn became a part of Hewlett-Packard. Regrettably, sales and service were not compatible with Mr. Olsen's definition of a company that wanted to make "the best computer in the industry."

2. **Leaders must *lead* the process of making strategy.** The foremost responsibility of senior leadership is to direct the enterprise to achieve its objectives. *Making* strategy, not just participating in the annual planning ritual, is too crucial to the success of the business to leave entirely to corporate planners or other staff members. And, to effectively lead the strategy-making process means that the executive must do more than simply rubber stamp or kill the planning work of others. A corollary responsibility of the executive is to be tolerant of the cauldron of ideas that can emerge from a culture that is conducive to challenging the existing order. The term *strategy*, in its full literal meaning, connotes "generalship" (the interrelatedness of the two terms is evident from its Greek antecedents: "strategy" is rendered as *stratigiki;* "general" as *stratigos*), as only generals have a full view and appreciation of the theater of war. The strategy-making process, therefore, cannot be led by staff or consultants; it must be led from the front by those at the top.

3. **Leaders must build a culture of service, a culture which fundamentally rests on a foundation of integrity.** Culture— the basic beliefs, values, and customs under which the organization operates—plays a major role in the business performance of a company. An ethic of service, in turn, springs from a culture where the customer is king. Flying pennants from the office tower or running around with shirt buttons that say "Service" fall way short of fostering the service ethic.

   A corporate culture with a clear focus on the customer goes far beyond a call to make money for the organization. Its focus is not inward toward production processes but outward toward the customer and the community at large. The process of cultural definition or redefinition, as the case may be, begins by articulating a clear mission objective. The companies I have led, for instance, have abided by a mission statement explicitly stating their corporate priorities: "*Customers are first. We will provide service to ensure the highest level of customer satisfaction.*" This statement is a call that summons the self to make a contribution on a morally higher plane than simply doing a job. Jim Clawson, professor at the University of Virginia Graduate School of Business Administration, calls such a mission a *service-oriented mission statement*. According to Clawson, this way of thinking about and presenting the organization's mission is intrinsically uplifting and energizing. Most people feel larger when they are a part of a morally powerful and serving purpose.[7] (Later in this book we will see how often a commitment to the customer is made in unequivocal terms by examining other companies' mission statements. Hint: If you haven't guessed, you will be disappointed.)

A culture of service can only thrive in an environment of truth telling and facts-based decision making if the root cause of a service issue is to be surfaced and corrected. A company afraid to deal with the facts out of respect for sacred cows or for fear of taking on a powerful internal political faction will chase at windmills and never get to the issue at hand. A company's executive leadership, therefore, requires the moral fortitude to champion the cause of honesty, equity, and fairness. Financial success—or success in any other context—while skimping on integrity is not an option. Here's how two companies responded in the face of serious challenges to the integrity of their organizations.

Toyota's problem over the sudden acceleration lurches of eight of its models, publicly acknowledged in October 2009, might not have reached the nightmarish proportions it did—the call to 911 by the driver of a runaway Lexus moments before he and three other people in the car were killed are still seared in our minds—had the company been more forthcoming when customers first complained of the problem. It turns out that Toyota learned about the throttle defect as early as 2004 but repeatedly pointed the finger at drivers and issues with floor mats as the real cause of the problem.[8] Meanwhile, in an unrelated case, a terminated product liability lawyer for Toyota claimed that the company failed to disclose information to litigants in personal injury cases on the nature of a number of roll-over accidents involving the automaker's SUV's and trucks.[9] The problem for Toyota was not so much whether the vehicles in question were defective—engineering defects are common in the manufacture of all complex products, and automobile recalls in particular number in the many tens of thousands. The bigger question and one that goes to the ethical foundation of the company is whether the leadership chose to thumb its nose at its customers, critics, and the government in the face of repeated safety concerns about its vehicles.

Major General Perry Smith, before he went to work at CNN as a military analyst during the first Persian Gulf War, had a brilliant career in the U.S. Air Force. General Smith was a fighter pilot during the Vietnam War, commanded the F-15 fighter wing in Germany, served as the air force's top planner during President Reagan's administration, and became commandant of the National War College.

General Smith quit his job at CNN after failing to get the network's management to retract a bogus story about U.S. pilots dropping nerve gas on their own troops in Laos during the Vietnam War. I asked the general why he took the action he did. His reply was to the point: "Look, that story should never have aired but for the pressure to produce television ratings. I see it as a leadership failure because of all the qualities that a leader must posses, integrity is by far the most important."

Time will tell what damage, if any, will be suffered by the Toyota brand for its failure to be more open and transparent about its defective autos. As for CNN, which launched the all-news cable network thirty years ago, its ratings have steadily declined—the network has lost approximately 17 percent of its viewers in the last decade—and now find itself in last place behind its competitors.

4. **Leaders must build a frontline organization that is competent, well trained, and well supported.** Service leadership requires that executives do not buy into the concept of acceptable failure rates. Leaders must deliver the message that 100 percent reliability is not just feasible but is the only acceptable standard of service. But words alone are not enough. Leaders must consider the front line the precious resource of a service-focused organization. The organization must be aligned with the customer, and it must have the freedom to exercise a bias for action on the customer's behalf. Furthermore, senior leadership must allocate the necessary sums of capital for advanced information systems and technology, and for the selection, training, and rewarding of qualified frontline workers.

Executives must perform all of the above roles with roughly equal emphasis. A sense of balance is mandatory: too much emphasis on one role—perhaps reflecting the executive's leadership style or personal sense of mission—is just as ineffective as too little.

## A CUSTOMER FOCUS VERSUS A BLURRED VISION

Wachovia Bank, one of the largest banks in the nation, publicly, and with great fanfare, announced that it had made an investment of $100 million to upgrade frontline staff to better serve its customer base. Crowing about the recently released American Customer Satisfaction Index (ACSI), which showed Wachovia was ranked the number one bank for customer satisfaction, its chairman and CEO, G. Kennedy Thompson, had this to say: "Providing excellent customer service is a hallmark of our company, and this award is a testament to our success."[10] (Having personally witnessed the recalcitrance of some of the bank's executives in my business dealings with them, I read the news as only so much propaganda, but read on and come to your own conclusion.)

Meanwhile, the bank was processing unauthorized, unsigned check transactions from thousands of accounts; representing auction-rate securities—complex, illiquid debt instruments—as alternatives to liquid money-market funds; ignoring anti-money laundering federal guidelines; and selling negative amortization mortgages whose principal balance would *increase* if the customer chose the lowest payment option available. In the first instance, court documents show that bank executives knew of the fraudulent scheme that allowed telemarketers to steal hundreds of millions of dollars from unwary depositors but failed to stop it. The reason: telemarketers were a huge source of revenue for the bank.[11] As to the bank's sales practices of auction-rate securities and negative amortization mortgages, and its disregard for money laundering safeguards it is clear the intent was to deceive the consuming public while feathering its own nest. So much for the bank's investment in frontline staff!

Unless an enterprise is prepared to execute on all of the critical success factors, a sustainable competitive advantage is not likely to be achieved. Wachovia's experience is proof positive: In April 2008, Wachovia agreed to pay $144 million to settle claims—other claims and investigations are still outstanding—that it allowed telemarketers to bilk depositors.[12] In June 2008, Mr. Thompson was ousted (more than likely the CEO was ousted for the disastrous Golden West Financial acquisition in 2006 and the source of the bank's subprime mortgage imbroglio). In July 2008, the bank eliminated 11,000 jobs. In August 2008, regulators forced the bank to buy back $9 billion of auction-rate debt, pay a $50 million fine, and make no-interest loans to consumers hurt by the fraud.[13] In October 2008, the bank, a victim of the subprime mortgage implosion it had a huge hand in inducing, got its comeuppance for its systemic cheating as it was picked over by both Citigroup and Wells Fargo. In the end, Wells Fargo prevailed by offering $11.7 billion for a bank that was worth *ten times* that amount only one year earlier. Wachovia consummated its deal with Wells Fargo only by spurning an earlier, exclusive deal it had struck with Citigroup, which surely will sue for as much as $60 billion for breach of contract.[14] Finally, in March 2010, Wachovia agreed to pay $160 million to the U.S. government for failing to block Mexican currency exchange houses from laundering billions of dollars—including drug-trafficking proceeds through the bank.[15]

This was a fitting coda to an abysmal leadership and ethical performance!

A leader's role is to drive his organization—indeed drive himself—in a direction that will ensure that the topmost corporate priority is, uncompromisingly, nothing less than that *customers are first.*

## THE PRINCIPAL LEADERSHIP CHALLENGE: OVERCOMING INERTIA

The role of executive leadership as change agents in any environment or circumstance is difficult enough. The leadership that seeks to fundamentally change the organization's service behavior, however, may encounter so much resistance that, in the end, all efforts at substantive change are frustrated. This is no small reason why the quest for excellence in service remains a dead letter with most organizations. What I call *antiservice biases* may manifest themselves in both overt ways as well as in fifth-column—clandestine internal resistance—efforts designed to preserve the status quo. Here are some of the biases and impediments that can derail a company's service efforts:

1. **A failure to issue a mandate from the top.** The organization's vision for the future must be understood to represent a mandate that emanates from executive leadership. This is a key requirement for service strategies to succeed. There is no other viable way, for the message has to be clear, unequivocal, and full of conviction and promise. The message must also have the clout that can only come from executive leadership. Nothing as far reaching as a customer-focused cul-

ture will take hold in the organization without tenacious and persistent executive leadership.

The key tasks needed to effect change in the organization cannot be delegated to the planning, marketing, or service departments. Outside consultants are no better and are probably the worst choice to carry the message. Only senior leadership can preach credibly and show by its behavior and decisions that there is constancy to the organization's customer focus. In addition, leaders must carry their organization's service commitment directly to the customer. Leaders must stay close to their customers in various ways and deliver the service message personally at every opportunity.

2. **Culture is devilishly difficult to change.** A company's culture forms over time and with the passage of time becomes resistant to change: a mighty pathogen impervious to the latest antibiotic. Leaders must understand this phenomenon and recognize that to effect true cultural change, the past—its vision, mission, values, behaviors, symbols, and so forth—must be unwound. Corporate managers spend considerable time redrawing organizational charts in the mistaken belief that doing so effects substantive changes in organizational behaviors. Organizational cultures, however, are almost immune to personnel changes unless the changes are deep and widespread. Leaders must recognize, therefore, that a critical component of their job is cultural assessment, change, and sustainability, and that they are the principal actors in the drama that must necessarily unfold. I am convinced that Wachovia Bank's demise would have been averted had the prevailing culture been one of challenging executive misbehavior.

3. **The transition to a culture of service can become an administrative nightmare.** Surveys, committee meetings, forms, and reports all are needed in transition to a culture of service and thereafter, but they cannot be allowed to become ends in themselves. When these administrative processes are overemphasized—I've seen staff members get caught up in a vortex of paperwork while forgetting the service mission—a distraction from the goal of a true customer focus is likely. Contrariwise, the added administrative focus required to monitor service and customer satisfaction cannot be allowed to serve as a foil to dissuade the organization from pursuing its service initiatives.

4. **Validating the cost-benefit ratio of every service initiative or strategy is a surefire way to nullify an organization's customer focus.** The mother's milk of effective service management action is swift and decisive responsiveness. This need is not served well by project evaluation techniques reliant on financial measures such as payback period methods, return on investment (ROI), and discounted cash flow (DCF). These techniques are rooted in industrial-age models of efficiency and factory accounting. The justification process itself can become so involved—tapping the appropriate corporate department resources to participate in the evaluation; extracting prior period enterprise costs for comparison; engaging in the analytics of one or more methods of cost-benefit analysis; seeking the time, person, and place for permission to proceed to be granted; and so forth—that precious time is lost.

In addition, these approaches almost always (a) ignore opportunity costs—that is, the income foregone by a decision *not* made—(b) attach all manner of direct, indirect, and overhead costs to any new activity, whether these costs are relevant to the new activity or not; (c) attempt to arbitrarily quantify the intangible benefits of an initiative (try putting a dollar value on initiatives designed to improve customer satisfaction or enhanced competitiveness in the marketplace); and (d) force a common time horizon to which all costs and benefits must be mapped.

Profitability analysis alone will not render an effective judgment on the advisability of pursuing an investment to improve service. Service initiatives are generally characterized by having a stream of short-term, tangible costs and long-term, intangible benefits and will, therefore, have a great deal of difficulty overcoming a conventional cost-benefit screen if not tempered by intuition and common sense. Time spent on analysis to gain added precision, past the point where prudent judgment supports the need to act, delays the time to market to deploy a service initiative and thus *enhances* risk to the enterprise. Besides, nothing can ever be known with great exactitude until an initiative is in the field and its effects measured. Leaders, therefore, should be watchful for the presence of these—on the face of it rational—ultimately insidious biases, which can eat away at an organization's customer focus.

5. **Investments in service initiatives are difficult to defend during tough economic times.** Difficult financial stretches for the organization—a way of life for many start-ups—create special challenges for executive leadership. At our company, we were awarded a three-year, multimillion-dollar project only after having provided the customer a number of engineering and technical services over a period of many months without any compensation. The cash burn was so dramatic that many times we questioned the wisdom of continuing these efforts. The stress was, at times, unbearable, and it took great leadership on the part of our executives to keep an eye on the prize.

   Remember, the conventional way to judge the value of a management team is simply to look at the financials—never mind that the organization is sharpening its service edge and engendering customer trust and loyalty through its actions. As these service initiatives ordinarily do not have a direct and immediate positive impact on the bottom line, the pressure on the executive—from both inside and outside the enterprise—to dispense with these can be substantial. The strategic damage caused by such a move, however, can rarely be justified and should vigorously be resisted.

6. **Personal antipathies toward a service-focused environment might torpedo substantive changes in the organization.** Not everyone in the organization will see eye-to-eye on the need to become customer focused. Many will find it personally objectionable or professionally untenable—particularly if their power base is eroded—to abide such a culture. The worst-case scenario for the organization is to have square-peg human resources in round-hole positions insofar as service to the customer is concerned. The customer-focused organization must be driven by individuals who share an obligation to serve the customer. Those individuals who do not buy into that vision must be found other opportunities.

7. **Strategic-planning biases conspire against the customer.** Strategic-planning processes in most organizations are tone deaf to emerging customer needs. In fact, planning cycles in most enterprises are so insular that the perpetuation of current business models is almost assured. This bias can only change at the behest of executive leadership. (We will talk at

length about the biases inherent in the planning process and the options available to the enterprise in the next chapter.)

8. **Computer information systems can impede service to the customer.** A complex financial or operational software system implementation, as a rule, changes the way the organization conducts business—whether the change is meritorious or not is another matter as many systems have been known to be scrapped before ever seeing the light of day. These same systems, however, by virtue of their complexity and interdependencies across enterprise processes, can erect barriers that can thwart, dilute, or slow down the adoption of important customer-driven initiatives. If the enterprise seeks process improvements, business efficiencies, and improved controls from its system efforts—as well it should—these cannot come at the expense of customer-facing or support applications that provide flexibility and high service levels. In any showdown between efficient system processes, on the one hand, and system processes that allow for flexibility and responsiveness to the customer, on the other, the latter must always be declared the winner. In the end, senior executives cannot let systems dictate how to run the business.

Service leadership is more about engaging the organization in a *process of change,* in response to changes in customer needs and requirements, than in the attainment of hard benchmarks. This view flies in the face of the prevalent leadership mythology that expects the achievement of tangible goals—say, hitting the numbers—as the only test of successful leadership. Leaders who posses clarity of strategy with regard to service will more than likely, in the face of these and other biases, have to stand on conviction—even if they stand alone—and continue to maintain their organization's focus. "Resist your time, take a foothold outside it," is how Lord Acton, the great professor of history at Cambridge—and whose admission as a student to that university ironically was made impossible because of his Roman Catholic beliefs—characteristically put it.[16] This is sobering advice for the customer-focused leader.

### STREAMLINING THE ORGANIZATION FOR A CUSTOMER FOCUS

As we have seen, an organization's defense system can kill change—a change to a customer focus or any other change for that matter. The design of the organization—who reports to whom and how—can also conspire to subvert a customer focus. Remember, the customer-focused leader is not so much redirecting the organization's priorities as its power structure. It is inevitable that a transition to a customer-focused environment will change the locus of power in the organization. Ringmasters of old may feel—rightly or wrongly—a loss of stature or actual power. A CEO who invites a frontline worker to bring directly to her attention systemic service mishaps—bypassing the organization's chain of command—will rock the boat in a way that it has never been rocked before. New processes of decision making will, by design, bring with them new power relationships that executive leadership will need to sort out without compromising the organization's service focus.

Regardless, the customer-focused executive is wise to consider taking the following actions designed to make the organization more congruent with its customer focus:

1. **Shedding corporate activities that impede service.** The cycle times in all phases of business have been streamlined and compressed by the new metronome of the economy: the microprocessor. Nonvalue-added activities—special forms, procedures, approval to handle routine actions, meetings, and department-to-department shuffling of a problem—add to the overhead and take attention away from the customer.

   As John Kenneth Galbraith has noted, the modern day corporate culture "runs strongly to the shifting of problems to others—to escape from personal mental effort and responsibility."[17] There is consensus among business leaders that unnecessary functions of the corporate bureaucracy should be eliminated. These functions, the conventional wisdom goes, detract from the organization's true value creation activities. My experience has been, however, that most efforts to streamline the organization are crude and, not surprisingly, allow much waste to remain within the enterprise while cutting out valuable activities.

   The customer-focused organization is far more rigorous in its approach to the evaluation of what constitutes a value-added activity. Simply put, any activity that does not benefit the customer—and that is not otherwise required by law—should be summarily eliminated. Karl Albrecht and Ron Zemke in their book *Service America!* put it this way: "If you're not serving the customer, you'd better be serving someone who is."[18] This rule applied to the work of registered nurses in hospitals, for example, would lead to dramatic improvements in patient care. How so? It has been estimated that nurses spend between one-third and two-thirds of their time on work other than caring for patients! If this isn't enough reason to reengineer the work of the registered nurse, consider that nurses have to deal with terribly stressful work conditions that include extended work hours (the result of a near universal state of understaffing in hospitals), high turnover, modest wages, and shift work. It is no wonder that the principal caregiver in health care—and prime arbiter of a patient's perception of hospital service and quality—is also the most dissatisfied employee on a hospital staff.[19]

A sensible approach to shedding nonvalue-added activities is not as difficult to implement as one might think: you would be surprised at how on the mark the efforts of the rank and file can be at eliminating irrelevant activities once the objective is clearly understood by all.

2. **Shortening the distance to the customer.** Corporate layers that impede service to the customer have no place in the customer-focused organization. The late 19th-century German sociologist, economist, and political scientist Max Weber aptly described the system of organization prevalent in the industrial age. Weber described an organization—a bureaucracy—where expertise, authority, and decision making were arranged in a hierarchy—the higher the perch of the office holder, the greater the concentration of these qualities.[20] In the service and information age, the days of the hierarchical and vertical form of organization are numbered—though this form of organization is still very much a force to be reckoned with. Vertical bureaucratic organizations cannot substitute mass for flexibility, size for responsiveness.

Information technology in combination with demographic, social, and political shifts has made obsolete the centralized bureaucracy with its rigid division of labor. Networked communications, inherently diffused as they are, have challenged the existence of command and control and the conceit that only at the top are important things knowable. The networked organization is, for all practical purposes, devoid of a center of gravity. Shortening the distance from the executive suite to the front line, and therefore to the customer, is a crucial requirement for the customer-focused organization. This requirement can only be effectively met with a flat, flexible, and nonbureaucratic organization in place.

3. **Opening multiple channels of communication**. Leaders cannot be effective with only formal channels as their principal tool of communication. This is true generally speaking but especially so when it comes to service interactions and customer feedback. This information, depending on its criticality, must be dealt with in real time. The customer-focused leader cannot afford to have important service information be delayed as it wends its way through formal channels. Neither should the leader put great stock in information that has been unduly filtered by middle-management ranks. There isn't a management information report in the world that will substitute for having a dialogue with the front line, or better, with the customer. Leaders need to hear firsthand what actions they might take to maintain their organization's customer focus.

    Additionally, leaders need to be accessible and open to anyone who needs help in serving the customer. Employees are hesitant to approach senior management if they think that their bosses are too busy to interact with them. The importance of cross-functional communication cannot be overstated in pursuing a customer-focused strategy. Open access to anyone who can help in serving the customer needs to be nurtured within the organization. At the same time, customers must be made aware of this attitude so that they are comfortable in accessing not just frontline people, but anyone from the supplier organization who may be of help.

3. **Devolving power to the front line**. The bedrock for sustained creative contributions by employees requires that leaders act on a deep-down belief in the potential of every person to contribute to the good of the organization by serving the customer. This means giving people the power to act, and the chance to experiment, and of necessity, to fail. The freedom to make decisions must be pushed down to the point where the customer most often interacts with the organization. To empower the workforce, leaders have to redefine their own risk-taking behavior. Errors of empowered employees have to be identified, not for punitive actions, but for the opportunity to learn to do better in the future. Given the variety and specificity of service encounters, it is very difficult to identify

each encounter and prescribe proper behavior in each case. In fact, the greater the uncertainty of the task, the more freedom the front line should have to act.

According to Jan Carlzon, who as president of Scandinavian Airlines did so much to bring the company back from the brink, people far out on the line, where the action is, must be given the authority to act. Carlzon asked his front line to think of every interaction with a customer as a "moment of truth." These moments, which Carlzon figured lasted on average 15 seconds, required the frontline worker to take responsibility for meeting the customer's needs right there and then.[21] These rapid-fire customer interactions simply did not allow time for consulting a manual or for checking in with headquarters. What is the lesson here? The front line must be given the clout to in effect be customer driven not rules driven.

Organizational inertia will kill innovation before it sees the light of day. The strongest defense you'll hear from an enterprise—especially those enjoying the current limelight—will always sport a tinge of hubris: "This has worked for us in the past; why change?"

What has changed indeed? The parry, of course, is all the more potent: truly revolutionary product and service ideas come not from industry incumbents—no matter how mighty—but from new or recent entrants who eschew the status quo.

## LEADERS MUST *LIVE* THEIR OWN MANDATE

Our company once competed for a large computer outsourcing contract that was up for renewal with a chemical company in Sao Paolo, Brazil. The chemical company was being serviced by outsourcing giant EDS who had operations literally across town. We felt disadvantaged as our business was located in Omaha, Nebraska, at the time. Still, we marketed hard. Several executives and I made repeated trips to our prospect in an effort to discount the distance factor. After many months of marketing, we were awarded a multiyear contract. EDS executives, in disbelief, appealed the decision to the customer's executive staff. To this day, the response by the customer executive in charge still rings loud. "Look," he said to EDS, "I've been your customer for years, and this is the very first time any of you have paid me a visit. I'm sorry, my decision is made. I've awarded the business to another company."

A leader's handiwork must be evident in everything a company does to make operational its customer focus. I mean everything. From articulating and executing a corporate mission, where the commitment to service and quality is made to the customer in no uncertain terms, to the creation and nurturing of a culture of service to the customer, to sponsoring—spearheading—the funding for quality- and service-related initiatives, to putting in place a corporate organization aligned with the customer and with a bias for action, to the way the company selects, trains, and rewards its employees to ensure a customer-focused attitude.

Employees and customers will infer a leadership's priorities by how they spend their time, how they allocate resources, and how they reward subordinates. Leadership in the service and information age is less about the management of things and tasks. Effective leadership today is all about successfully dealing with and managing human relationships both inside and outside of the enterprise in uncertain contexts. An effective leader is buoyant, although realistic; workmanlike, although playful; full of laughter and fun, although serious of purpose; and aggressive in the pursuit of business, but always ethical. These attributes can elicit mirrorlike responses from workers who want to find common cause with their leader.

I know the CEO of a publicly traded technology services company who went years between trips to visit workers at the company's one plant. An accountant by trade, the man was detached and always felt more comfortable in the familiar surroundings of his executive suite; he rarely spoke to his CFO, who happened to occupy the adjoining office! Clearly, he had no power base among the executive staff or the rank and file. Worst of all, this executive rarely paid a visit to his customers. The CEO was eventually swept away by his board of directors, but not because it did not appreciate his aloof and reclusive manner—an attitude which had been on display for all to see for many years—but because investors disapproved of the erosion of the company's stock price. (Given the persistence of industrial-age views, I have no doubt that the CEO's hermitlike behavior would have been long tolerated had the company's stock price held up.)

A leader's role is to leave his signature on a company's public and private statements, its structure, and its plans and actions with respect to service and quality. Most importantly, effective leaders are those who are never afraid to lead by example. Unfortunately, the leadership style that prevails today is timid, dour, and rigid.

Contemporary leadership is informed more by political correctness and the fear of making mistakes than by the vision to accomplish something truly transformative. (In chapter 3, we will talk about how the regulatory climate in the country is further sapping assertiveness from business leaders.)

When the $38 billion London-based grocery retailer Sainsbury's e-commerce site, used by customers to order merchandise that is subsequently delivered to their homes, went down for a period of 48 hours, the company's staff called some 30,000 customers to *personally* apologize and to offer them a $20 voucher.[22] Needless to say, that kind of service recovery initiative did not come out of a customer service manual. More likely, it was the result of an enlightened service leadership style that was courageous and convicted to do the right thing by the customer.

## THE GREATEST SERVICE STORY EVER TOLD

I met Bill McGowan in Washington, D.C., on two different occasions in the 1980s. One of these visits was strictly social; the other, all business. I didn't know it then, but with the passing of time, it has become clear that here was a man who brought together unique leadership attributes to forge not just a new enterprise but a whole new industry based on service to the customer. This story could not be told were it not for the vision, strength of character, conviction, and entrepreneurial instincts of McGowan.

McGowan, with cofounder Jack Goeken, was the man responsible for the launch in 1968 of Microwave Communications Inc., a company with a plan to construct microwave towers to carry radio transmission for use between truckers and their dispatchers on the route between St. Louis and Chicago. A service such as the one Mr. McGowan and his partner envisioned could have been provided by AT&T with its vast resources at the drop of a hat, but that was not to be. What came to be known as MCI Communications Corporation, a $20 billion revenue company before its merger with Worldcom, is the best example I know that describes what is possible when strong leadership drives a customer-focused vision. MCI, financially on the ropes for many of its early years, was held together by the glue that was McGowan's tenacity. A lesser leader would have been felled by AT&T's fair and unfair practices—a favorite of which was to disconnect MCI's circuits to its customers—designed to crush the impudent upstart.

When Mr. McGowan decided to launch MCI, all that stood in his way was AT&T, a company that controlled nearly 100 percent of the long-distance market in the United States, and the Federal Communications Commission (FCC), whose bureaucrats could not—or would not—understand why there was a need to have another telecommunications provider in the country. In the end, Mr. McGowan's vision led to the break up of AT&T in 1984 and nothing short of a revolution in the field of telecommunications, which continues to this day with far-reaching benefits for all consumers.

Our company signed a joint venture agreement with MCI for the purpose of offering enterprise customers telecommunications and computing services as a package. The motivation for our company to strike an alliance with MCI was the need that we understood—a need shared by MCI—was not being met by suppliers in the marketplace for a bundled service offering. At the time, computing and telecommunications companies were each going their separate ways. Our choice of MCI as a prospective partner was based on what we knew of the company's entrepreneurial drive to satisfy the needs of the customer. We were vindicated in our choice of partner. As Lorraine Spurge says in her book tracing the history of MCI, "AT&T developed technology through its Bell Labs division, *then* (italics mine) brought it to market. Conversely, MCI listened to what consumers wanted."[23] As Ms. Spurge goes on to say, "By staying in touch with what people from all walks of life thought, wanted, and needed, McGowan was able to match MCI's products with the diverse needs of consumers."[24]

As someone who has negotiated literally dozens of alliance and joint venture transactions, I was struck at how quickly MCI was able to conclude a deal with us after the idea was broached with the company. Few meetings and less red tape delivered an agreement in record time. That MCI was able to wrap up a deal with us so quickly was vintage McGowan. In her book Lorraine Spurge came to the same conclusion: "One of MCI's greatest corporate strengths has always been its willingness to try new things—and to quickly abandon them if they don't succeed. The essence of the company's management style is flexibility."[25]

McGowan died an untimely death at the age of 64 in 1992. He was thus unable to witness the signing of the Telecommunications Act of 1996, ending government regulation over local and long-distance telecommunications almost 30 years after he began his battle with the AT&T behemoth. Clearly, that was Mr. McGowan's principal legacy. The merger of MCI and Worldcom in 1997 might have been right up his alley, too, as it provided consumers one-stop shopping for all their telecommunications needs. In contrast, the eventual bankruptcy of Worldcom in 2002, following massive fraud that involved inflating revenues and underreporting costs, was one of the worst examples of a company that had lost its way without an ethical, visionary, and strong leader at the helm.

## COMING FULL CIRCLE

The hallmark of the customer-focused leader is the personal conviction and belief that customer needs and requirements are the principal driver of enterprise actions in the service and information age. This core belief is not an expression of subservience to the customer; it is just plain, good business. (We will address this issue at length in chapter 3 in our discussion on the ethics of service.)

Anyone can be in charge. Almost anyone, perhaps, can assume a position of leadership; few, however, can be said to be customer-focused leaders. The founder of Digital Equipment Corporation (DEC), Ken Olsen, certainly succeeded in the launch of the minicomputer juggernaut "the old-fashioned way." The company, in many ways, was founded along the fault line between the industrial age and the service and information age in the late 1950s. Nonetheless, DEC was able to survive into the 1990s, giving Mr. Olsen and the company ample opportunity to adapt to the emerging ascendancy of the customer. In the end, he didn't adapt, and neither did the company.

The contrast with the leadership style of MCI's McGowan could not be more stark. Successful in the launch of a new business that presaged a new industry, as in Mr. Olsen's case, the difference in the two leaders was that Mr. McGowan intuitively understood that listening to the customer unleashed a unique source of differential market power. Mr. McGowan fully embraced this view; Mr. Olsen ignored it, if not scoffed at it. In the end, Mr. McGowan's view proved to have sustainability.

If, as I suggested at the opening, mediocre service has become institutionalized in many organizations, it is largely the result of a play-it-safe, pusillanimous leadership style. I also believe, however, that *excellence* in service can become just as habit forming. That state of affairs is premised, first and foremost, on executive leadership that can lead with alacrity, energy, honesty, and courage.

# A Customer Focus Trumps All Other Strategies

The purpose of business is to get and keep a customer.
—*Theodore Levitt*
*The Marketing Imagination*

Recently, I stayed at a Hilton hotel during a business visit. As I was checking out, the desk clerk asked me, "So, how was everything?" I said, "Well, everything was satisfactory except for breakfast this morning. I don't like a cold breakfast that is supposed to be hot!" She promptly quipped, presumably a reflex of her training, "Would you kindly fill out this customer feedback form?" "No!" I said, "That is hardly the kind of satisfaction I was seeking." Eventually, and only after having put up a fuss, did the clerk offer to remove the breakfast charge from the bill. Nonetheless, I was stunned; more stunned than angry that—as Jan Carlzon would say—a valuable "moment of truth" had been squandered by a frontline worker at one of the premier hospitality chains in the world. And, regrettably, an opportunity at service recovery—turning lemons into lemonade—had been lost forever.

Why does this happen? We would all like to believe that my experience was anecdotal—an exception to the rule. It is not. Stories like these are a common occurrence. Organizations, including otherwise very sophisticated corporations, mistakenly believe that they are attuned to the customer. Unfortunately, the opposite is closer to the truth.

The problem extends beyond the world of business. Many universities lose more than 30 percent of their freshman and sophomore students. So what do these universities do to deal with the problem? They appoint a director of student retention! Reactive, patchwork solutions abound in spite of their failure to show any significant positive results.

In this chapter, we will discuss how classic strategic planning has failed to be the source of innovative, customer-centric business strategies with the consequence that we are congealed in time with a geocentric theory of strategy formation that is refuted by the facts.

## THE WINDS OF CHANGE FAVOR THE CUSTOMER

In the aftermath of World War II, mass production became the foundation of the U.S. economy. By 1967, in his book, *The Industrial State*, John Kenneth Galbraith disabused readers of the notion that consumers operating through the market had any part in deciding what was to be produced. So concerned was Professor Galbraith by what he observed as the consumer's powerlessness that he was moved to remark that our economic system "whatever its formal ideological billing, is in substantial part a planned economy."[1] Some 40 years later, this has all changed as the balance of power now lies firmly with the customer.

This is due in large measure to several techno/economic trends born of the age in which we now live:

- **The world economy is accelerating rapidly.** According to the National Intelligence Council, the world economy is projected to grow by 80 percent in the period that spans the years 2000 to 2020. During the same period, global per capita incomes are expected to be roughly 50 percent higher.[2] A rapidly growing middle class on the world stage means a huge explosion of consumption and commensurately huge power in the hands of consumers.
- **Geography is dead.** The cliché itself is resurrected each time there appears on the scene a dramatic improvement in transportation or communication. But never before have truth and rhetoric so tightly converged. High-speed communications access now allows consumers to traverse time and distance as never before. The broadband revolution makes this possible to the consumer at little or no cost. The upshot: consumers— admittedly presently distributed unevenly throughout the world's regions and highly concentrated in the developed economies—now have better and cheaper access to market-

place information anytime, anywhere. Globalization is inexorable despite the screams of the antigrowth, so-called nongovernmental organizations (NGOs). (I say so-called because these organizations all have political agendas, and many are government sponsored.)

- **E-commerce has become pervasive.** The transparency brought on by the Internet allows producers and consumers to be connected directly and thus transact all manner of business one to one. This process of disintermediating the middleman is taking place not just in manufacturing—jeopardizing the viability of wholesalers and distributors as we know them today—but in service industries as diverse as hospitality, financial services, health care, and government services.

- **The customer has become more demanding than at any other time in the history of the world economy.** According to the previously cited customer satisfaction survey conducted by Accenture, consumers report that they have higher service expectations today than they did one year ago, never mind five years ago. The consumer's powerlessness, which Professor Galbraith was so fearful of in a prior age, has been supplanted by a consumer confident that his product needs, no matter how unique, can be met. And woe be to the provider that ignores claims of defective product or slipshod service: the Internet can work its magic in reverse by allowing aggrieved consumers to pillory merchants for millions of fellow consumers to see. The good news here is that new product design technologies, advanced manufacturing techniques, and competition from all corners of the globe now allow for blinding diversity in product and service options.

- **The new competitiveness in the world economy is squeezing producer prices and margins.** In a world of commoditized product choices and lower prices, a supplier's ability to become differentiated from the pack will turn not so much on product superiority or price but on service superiority. Service quality and customer satisfaction will be important arbiters of how successful enterprises can be in attracting and retaining customers in the new economy.

In sum, in the service and information age, it is fanciful—perilous—to craft a business strategy that is not at heart a customer-focused strategy. You don't believe me? Compare the *Fortune* 500 list in 1967 and the *Fortune* 500 list today. More than half of the companies thriving in 1967 are no longer in business. Why? The simple reason is because customers stopped buying their products and services sufficiently to keep the company viable. And, with the accelerating pace of societal and business change, it might not take nearly as long as 40 years for 50 percent of the companies from the current list to vanish.

## STRATEGIC PLANNING CANNOT YIELD STRATEGY

Strategic planning has evolved and matured over the last 50 years to the point that nearly every organization, large or small, can claim to follow a formal planning process to a greater or lesser extent. Some companies—especially large companies operating in mature industries—have planning processes that are highly elaborate and complex. Small companies and others operating in turbulent industries might combine process rigor with a dose of intuition. No two companies approach strategic planning in exactly the same way—one size does not fit all—but most companies work within the same general framework.

Yet it has never been clear that strategy can emanate from a strategic-planning process. F. A. Hayek, Nobel laureate in economics, said that knowledge of economic circumstances—Hayek was speaking of economic circumstances at a societal level, but the point is relevant nonetheless—never exists in concentrated form. The great economist went on to say that the knowledge necessary for planning is never given to the planner but to somebody else.[3] The point Hayek is making is that planners have to *elicit* the necessary knowledge from those who possess it.

Professor Henry Mintzberg, who has written on management and business strategy for more than 40 years, has labeled the term *strategic planning* an oxymoron.[4] That being the case, how *do* we (1) formulate strategy and (2) formulate strategy around a customer's needs and requirements. We'll attempt to address those issues subsequently, but, for now, let's review, at a high level, what we know of the sequence of steps in the contemporary practice of strategic planning:

1. **Statement of objectives.** Almost every company starts their planning cycle by having senior management state its objectives for the coming year or other planning horizon. In

large companies, objectives might be set after consultation between top management and divisional chiefs who presumably have a greater depth of knowledge of the operations of the business. Also, constituencies such as labor unions, institutional shareholders, lenders, or industry research analysts might be the source of data points that influence corporate management's stated objectives.

Key national or international economic forecast data, despite their manipulation by government to satisfy narrow political interests, and suspect always in measuring true economic performance, are heavily relied on for the formulation of objectives (for a terrific article depicting this economic sophistry in the hands of government read "The Erosion of Trust—CPI and GDP Distorted for Political Purposes").[5] The gross domestic product (GDP), housing starts, the consumer price index (CPI), the cost of crude oil, interest rates, the rate of unemployment, and so on can influence the derivation of objectives for the coming planning season by the strength or direction of their expected values. Revenue and earnings growth, gross margin targets, and return on investment expectations usually lead the parade of objectives that will drive the planning process. Some companies have as their objectives improvements in plant capacity utilization or labor productivity. In industries where the data are available, these objectives can be supplemented by more macro measures such as expected market share gains. Almost always, these objectives are some function—plus or minus, but usually plus—of the previous planning period's numbers. In some cases, the feedback loop in a tightly managed planning process allows for a stated objective to be amended after its initial issuance, but by and large, these objectives are understood as given.

Despite their apparent diversity, objectives that feed the planning process generally have two attributes in common: First, they are top down. Whether stated objectives are the result of negotiation and consensus with divisional chiefs or not, the fact remains that objectives emanate from executive offices high on the organizational chart and thus fail to leverage the potential for innovative thinking that might reside deep in the organization. Objectives thus derived are not so much trial balloons that should be put to the test, and subsequently either discarded or applied, but very much like mandates that the downstream planning process must abide. Second, objectives are mostly quantitative or financial measures of expected performance. Objectives might be the result of a forecasting scheme involving a great deal of mathematical manipulation and precision, but that does not change the character of the objective, only how its numeric value is computed. In the end, most objectives are stated as a number—or a bracketed set of numbers to account for most likely, optimistic, or pessimistic outcomes.

Trying to understand the future in the most stable environments means dealing with a staggering number of variables. In the service and information age, uncertain environments are the rule and not the exception. Contingency planning is the recent darling of management consultants and academics frustrated with the inefficacy of current planning regimens. But, the crafting of alternate strategies based on alternate future outcomes won't be of much help either. The pervasive uncertainty brought about by the service and information age makes crafting alternate strategies to deal with alternate scenarios little more than chasing at windmills. Practically speaking, can any organization's strategic-planning process deal with multiple scenarios except at a conceptual level? And, if scenarios are considered only conceptually, does that really help the organization improve its readiness for the contingent future? Other practical concerns abound. For instance, how does the organization choose how many scenarios to build? Does each scenario demand its own contingent strategy response? It is one thing to *imagine* a scenario; it is quite another to craft a strategy in response. Once the plausible range of scenarios has been identified, does one scenario become favored over others? If so, the chosen outcome is no longer *contingent* but rather the *expected* outcome on which presumably corporate strategies will be built. Finally, if a scenario is sufficiently out of the box, will it be taken seriously?

Churning out better, more accurate forecasts of expected corporate performance is the key output at this stage of the strategic-planning process. Despite all of the forecasting machinations, however, the future refuses to be forecast with consistent accuracy. In the end, the principal business challenge remains—namely, what *direction* to take the business in the light of forecasts and predictions.

2. **Environmental scan.** A scan of the environment is the next input to the planning process. The environmental scan or analysis seeks to identify: (1) the firm's strengths and weaknesses, and (2) the opportunities and threats facing the firm in its macro environment. Such a scan conducted both inside and outside the firm is referred to as a SWOT (*s*trengths, *w*eaknesses, *o*pportunities, and *t*hreats) analysis and has as its purpose the mapping of the firm's attributes to the known or expected phenomena in the marketplace. An environmental scan, depending on the planner's appetite, can be far reaching and include a survey of those social, legal, technological, political, and economic factors or forces that can facilitate or impede an organization's success in the marketplace. Some companies reverse the order of this step of the planning process with the previous planning step so that objectives are not stated until the SWOT analysis is completed.

    Coming to terms with a company's competitive stance vis-à-vis existing or anticipated market forces has compelling value and thus requires participation by executive leadership. Much of the value of this process step, however, is nullified if it is conducted in the context of a planning activity and not an *intelligence gathering* activity. The difference is fundamental: the former is a slave to the planning calendar; the latter is continuous as emerging trends of consequence may require an immediate corporate response. Second, it isn't clear that emerging trends—*prototrends*, really—can be discerned through a systematic analysis of the environment. Market forces that are identified through analysis are historical by definition and thus are hardly dynamic or emerging. Finally, the assessment of what constitutes an enterprise strength or weakness, threat or opportunity can leave much room for interpretation and so should be the subject of a healthy leadership debate and not be relegated to an econometric exercise.

3. **Strategy formulation.** In theory, strategies can be inferred at this stage of the planning process. Product strategies, marketing strategies, financial strategies, and so forth all are presumed to be lodged in the planning process at the ready and waiting to be identified. How do we tease these

brilliant strategies from three-ring binders full of planning documents? This is where the wheels come off the planning bus!

Strategy formulation is an art; it takes intuition, creativity, and imaginative thinking; it takes knowing what questions to ask. The point is that strategy is not likely to be a product of the planning process per se. Professor Mintzberg suggests that this is the result of a logical contradiction inherent in the planning process: strategic planning is essentially an analytical process; strategy formulation—or as Professor Mintzberg refers to it, *strategy formation,* to emphasize the spontaneity of the process—is all about synthesis.[6] A plan, therefore, is orderly, mathematical, and rational; a strategy is visionary and intuitive.

4. **Implementation of strategies**. Implementation of the chosen strategies is the final step of the planning process. This step begins by decomposing strategies into substrategies and sub-substrategies until there has been created actionable-sized chunks of strategy that the organization can reasonably be expected to implement throughout divisions and departments. Depending on the size and complexity of the organization, these substrategies can exist at the corporate, divisional, and functional levels. Functional substrategies are those that direct the activities of departments such as marketing, finance, or manufacturing.

The analytical slicing and reslicing of strategy is meant to facilitate comprehension by the organization and the subsequent development of divisional or departmental performance objectives. The downside of the process, however, is that most times strategy *is* complex, and to attempt to atomize it runs the very real risk of oversimplifying important nuances that can compromise strategy formation.

Operational plans and budgets that stem from the strategic-planning process are almost always out of step with strategy from day one. Budgeting has always been more about hitting the numbers than facilitating the execution of strategy. It is impossible for budgeting to serve these two masters. In the service and information age, a fixation with budgets will surely compromise strategy. A customer of ours had a strategic vision to revolutionize patient care by introducing an interactive video system of education and entertainment under full patient control. A three-year plan to roll out the visionary system was aborted after three months because the system was costing more than expected. The system had demonstrated dramatic improvements in patient satisfaction and exhibited an attractive return on investment. No matter. The company preferred to interrupt its vision than to miss the numbers.

The planning process described above was a product of its time: analysis incarnate. Some believe that the strategic-planning process we have outlined is about more than planning—that it is a philosophy, an attitude, a way of thinking.[7] As for me, I don't believe strategic planning as practiced today is anything more than it is: a bureaucratic process where the focus is *process* in lieu of meaningful *action*. The following account is an example of what I mean.

The first information technology service company I had the privilege to lead was capitalized in the early 1980s by National Intergroup (NII), a holding company whose principal asset was the National Steel Corporation. This company had witnessed for decades—as others in the steel industry did as well—the erosion of their markets from substitute products (e.g., aluminum for tin plate), the decline of steel-intensive finished products, and cheap-labor-based imports. The company's management eventually recognized the threat, but it was too little, too late. In 1979 the company purchased a savings and loan association in a misguided attempt to diversify, and four years later, it financed our start-up on not much more than a shoestring. The diversification was reversed a scant three years later when 20 percent of the savings and loan business was spun out. Still, *30 years* after reaching peak production volumes for raw steel, this company was still going through its planning ritual, in effect whistling past the graveyard. (In the 21st century, the domestic steel industry continues to operate at 80 percent of the production volumes attained in the 1950s!) I remember participating in planning meetings where the principal discussion item was trying to fathom Detroit's expected auto and truck output as a way to *back into* National's steel production objective for the coming year. The rest of the story is not a pretty one.

In 1984, 50 percent of National Steel was sold to Japanese steel maker Nippon Kokan—an additional 20 percent was sold in 1990. In 1985 the company had to fend off a nasty proxy challenge by Leucadia National to replace four directors on NII's board. Also in 1985, the rest of the savings and loan business was sold, and in 1990, our technology service business was also sold. That our computer business was not seen as a long-term strategic asset proved to be a blunder of epic proportions as the company's management held on to its industrial-age past in a final swan song. In 2002 NII was forced to declare bankruptcy.

## STRATEGIC PLANNING IS ALL ABOUT CONTROL

Frederick Taylor's decomposition of routine work tasks, standardization of methods, and decoupling of *work* tasks from *management* tasks was his contribution to what became known as *scientific management*[8]—another oxymoron? (Clearly Taylor wasn't practicing science when he suggested that an intelligent gorilla could handle the work of loading pig-iron more efficiently than a man!) Henry Ford came along later with standardized product offerings that facilitated mass production.[9] The two management innovations in combination made sure that efficient production processes outpaced demand. It thus became imperative for management to introduce order and control through a centralized planning process that allowed little, if any, wiggle room for quantum—sudden, creative, and dramatic—change. We have been in that planning treadmill ever since.

A careful study of the above discussion should lead the reader to conclude that whatever the benefits of strategic planning might have been in its historical context, it was not then, nor is it now, the process that can liberate strategy. On the contrary, the planning process by virtue of its formal, analytical, and control orientation almost guarantees that disruptive change is nullified. In other words, the planning process preserves the *existing* order at the expense of creative strategy formation.

The word *totalitarian* comes to mind: Castro, Mao, and Stalin all had failed regimes not so much because they were malefactors—which they were to the nth degree—but because their planning regimens brooked no outside influence. The last thing a CEO of an enterprise in the service and information age should wish to have visited on his company is a *homogeneous* mind-set in any aspect of his business.

Not even in the field of science with its bona fide demand for rigor does progress stem from a slavishly analytical stepwise process. Nobel laureate Richard Feynman, perhaps the greatest physicist of the second half of the 20th century (best known for having solved the riddle of the failed *Challenger* space shuttle by dunking an O-ring in ice water and then pounding it on the table to show it had become brittle), is said to have accomplished more through common sense than through computer models, more through insight than equations.[10]

## FINDING THE CUSTOMER'S VOICE

The character of the strategic-planning process as we know it—its linearity, its formalism, its regularity—makes hope the plan: a hope that the world with all its chaos, discontinuities, and instabilities can somehow be freeze-dried while the planners do their thing. The reality of strategy making is far messier that the mandarins in the planning department would have us believe. The sheer incrementalism of the strategic-planning process in place today ensures that new strategic initiatives are not breakthrough initiatives but incremental tweaks to existing strategy.

Strategy formation is not a consequence of strategic planning per se but of strategic visioning—visioning that springs from listening and learning. The organization's leadership must therefore create an environment—a culture—by which it enables listening and learning, not as part of an annual planning exercise but spontaneously and at all times.

A customer-centric, strategy-making process is dynamic, complex, and filled with ambiguity. It thus starts with the premise that all that is knowable about the customer at a particular point in time *cannot* be known with much exactitude. (This has to do as much with the difficulty of the process as with the fact that we as humans cannot always put into words what we know. As scientist and philosopher Michael Polanyi reminds us, the nature of knowledge is such that "we know more than we can tell.")[11] This premise is an important foundational element—albeit rarely recognized in business today—to the strategy-making process because it implies that there is no beginning or end. In other words, the process is circular. And, no degree of strategy-making success—a breakthrough, perhaps brought about by capturing some important insight—in our circular peregrinations should call for its finality. In the service and information age, strategies will have to evolve at blinding speed. No single strategic success, therefore, should be allowed to reintroduce organizational inertia. A strategic success, if anything, should be used as a launching pad for continued customer probing, which, in turn, might lead to new strategic thrusts.

How then do we go about finding the customer's voice? Where can we find such a voice that it can be factored into a strategy-making process? The *how* is not as important as the *where*. The former speaks to the mechanics of the process, which might be suitable for one organization, given its structure and resources, but not for another. Again, one size does not fit all. In its most rigid incarnation, however, it might be no less orderly, organized, and rigorous than the prevailing strategic-planning process that we have outlined above. The principal difference in the two is that customer needs and requirements—not an arbitrary set of short-term financial objectives—should catalyze a process that is continuous and not subservient to the calendar.

The answer to the second question is that the customer's voice, surprisingly, can be found in many places. The planning process simply needs to be adjusted so that it knows where to look. Here are some of the more likely places to find the customer's voice:

- **Visionary leaders within the organization.** Steven Jobs of Apple Computer is the quintessential visionary in the computing industry and thus has an instinctive sense of how his products can serve the needs of the customer. "We do no market research," says Mr. Jobs.[12] Principal founder of a company always on the cutting edge of design and aesthetics, Mr. Jobs was the visionary leader behind the much adulated Macintosh computer: the first successful entry into the marketplace for a computer with a graphical user interface (GUI)—though invented at Xerox PARC years earlier. The iPod digital music player, iTunes digital music software, iTunes Store, the display cell phone iPhone, and the iPad tablet computer all speak to his genius. A lot of people contributed to the success of these many products, but there is no gainsaying where the vision originated. (In the early 1990s, Apple did suffer a dismal failure with the introduction of its Newton, an early personal digital assistant (PDA) product. That product, however, was championed by former soda-pop marketer and then CEO of Apple John Sculley, and not Mr. Jobs who had by then left the company in a rift with his board.) Steven Jobs likes to use hockey great Wayne Gretzky's quotation that explains the sportsman's own genius: "I skate to the where the puck is going to be; not where it has been." This is a pithy comment that speaks tomes about visionary leadership.

- **Executives and frontline members of the organization.** Visionary leaders, like Mr. Jobs, are a statistical oddity. If a company has one, he should be given wide berth. For companies staffed with mere mortals, the challenge is to tap the potentially creative ideas that might be harbored in the most unlikely of places in the organization. Japanese companies have been very good at this—actually it is Japanese New-Confucianism that inculcates in the individual an ethic to improve himself and his team—by establishing an expectation with all workers that they should think and volunteer ways to improve the enterprise. Frontline workers, and sales executives, especially, interacting often as they do with customers, are a potential lodestone in identifying customer-focused initiatives and thus cannot remain passive participants in the strategy-formation process. Spontaneous feedback, in fact, might at times be more valuable—it can prove to be more timely—than the well-studied responses that might result from meetings, surveys, questionnaires, or focus groups administered by the enterprise.

  There are some important preliminaries that need to be in place, however, before the front line can become an effective conduit for sound customer-focused ideas. These considerations we address in detail in chapter 4—individual competence, empowerment, and system support. Suffice it to say that empowering the worker is especially vital in order to provide the individual the freedom to question long-held organizational approaches—without the fear of causing a self-inflicted wound that can ruin a career—and practices that may not appear to serve the customer well.

- **Current customers.** Not every customer is created equally, though each might have unlimited potential. The process of plumbing customers for feedback begins with an intelligent approach to the segmentation of the customer base. In our technology service business, for instance, the needs of equipment warranty service customers are very different from those of customers who need to have desktop computing technology refreshed at lease expiration time. The needs of these customers are different still from those whom we help in deploying high-speed wireless broadband. In financial services, the needs of the customer with a savings deposit are different from those with a mortgage, which in turn are different from those with an installment loan, a trust account, or a checking account. Segmentation along economic lines—customer profitability, size of account, and so forth—provides additional focus for understanding the needs of the customer. Further segmentation along demographic, geographic, behavioral, even psychographic (an individual's interests, attitudes, values, etc.) dimensions is advisable to affirm or dismiss that these factors make a difference in customer behavior.

Marketing to defined customer segments allows for nuanced strategies and initiatives that are not evident when analyzing coarsely aggregated data. In other words, without segmenting the customer base, it is not possible to launch product or service design initiatives that are firmly rooted to the customer experience. This segmentation is also crucial as a way to allocate scarce resources and focus on customer segments that afford maximum or most immediate leverage and payback. Once the customer set is properly segmented, the process of reaching out for opinion and feedback becomes the province of professionals engaged in the design, administration, and analysis of surveys and questionnaires.

- **Past customers**. Past customers hold the key to invaluable—potentially negative and thereby useful—information on the firm's track record in the marketplace. Why did the customer cancel his account? Was it the product, the price, the service, or other factors? What would it take to bring the customer back? Who handles the customer's business now? Why did the customer choose to do business with our competitor? Don't forget, most customers who are dissatisfied with our products or services never complain—giving us an opportunity to right a wrong—they just walk. Approaching lost customers might bring some of them back. And, even if they never return, the approach will be seen as a goodwill gesture that can nullify negative prior service experiences.
- **Future customers**. Prospects ordinarily approach a supplier—or in turn are approached by a supplier—with one product or service need that must be satisfied. It is a mistake often made, however, to fail to display the wider assortment of products and services offered by the firm: these additional service offerings might tip the balance and close the deal. Again, a battery of questions must be designed to elicit direct and relevant

customer feedback: What are the customer's specific needs? How do our products and services match his needs? What about our other products and services? Who else is the customer considering for his business? What does it take to win the customer's business?

Before we launched our computer outsourcing services company in the early 1980s, we listened carefully to what customers of established suppliers had to say. Among the many things that we learned, the one that especially stood out as a sore subject with customers was the prevailing industry practice of billing for computing resources consumed that proved almost impossible for the customer to forecast or budget. The typical monthly invoice was indecipherable as it was so replete with technical computer gobbledygook. Any resource in the computer center, if it could be measured, was metered, tariffed, and charged to the customer. The result was that invoices, even for medium-sized businesses, ran to 10, 20, or 30 pages. A cynic might say that the supplier's intent was to keep the customer in the dark so that charges could not easily be understood let alone challenged. Our company changed all of that by pioneering a single line—not a single page, but a single line—invoice. Simply stated, we learned how to bundle all of the resources consumed into a single unit of measure and to communicate that fact in simple English. Our approach to billing rendered our invoices easy to understand and to follow by the average business person. The new billing practice became an immediate success and an important differentiator that allowed our start-up company to compete with the big players in the industry.

Here is a different example from the world of education. College recruiters frequently call on me to hire graduates with computer degrees. I rarely do. When they ask me why I don't, I usually tell them that it is because the students are trained in many areas that are irrelevant to the work that we do in our company. I also tell recruiters that if the computer department chairman would call or visit, I would tell him exactly the kinds of course work that we would find most helpful and that more than likely would lead to our hiring more of their graduates. I have been called exactly *one* time. And on that occasion, the chairman explained that professors like to teach *their* competencies! Imagine how successful a commercial enterprise would be if it took this take-it-or-leave-it attitude. (This disdain by the priesthood in higher education to satisfy the needs of the customer is not universal. Contrast this attitude with my far more refreshing experience at the University of Limerick in Ireland later in the book.)

- **Transactional systems.** Purposely last on our list is access to customer data resident in enterprise sales or service computer system databases or data warehouses. The principal advantage to what in today's parlance is referred to as *data mining* is that it has the potential to unleash large amounts of customer data for analysis that might reveal important patterns of consumer behavior and do so relatively cost effectively. On the other hand, warehoused data reflects *past* patterns of consumer behavior and thus may offer few clues to current or prospective buyer behavior. Also, whether the sampled data can be used to predict the behavior of an entire population is a matter for the professional statistician. In any event, suspected patterns of behavior must be confirmed through other research methods such as customer surveys. Finally, patterns of behavior may not be discernible at all if the data has not been properly collected, organized, and stored for extraction and reporting.

A comment should also be made about the current practice of competitive analysis. Sir Winston Churchill famously said, "When making plans, it is well to take into account those of the enemy."[13] Competitive analysis for our purposes is not so much to learn what the enemy is doing in order to design a counterstrategy—to be sure a valid and important enterprise function—but to learn why a potential customer of ours chooses to do business with the competition. We might have a good idea who our competition is from regulatory filings, press releases, Web sites, third-party services, and our own sales force. These sources, too, might avail us the necessary information to conduct analytical studies comparing our company's products, services, or pricing with those of the competition. Competitive analysis, however, is not a substitute for the direct surveying of a customer population. That is the subject of our next section.

## CUSTOMER SURVEY DESIGN AND ADMINISTRATION

Survey design is as much art as it is science. The art involves the proper wording of survey questions to ensure they are not confusing, ambiguous, vague, biased, or leading. What we want to know from the customer, among other things, includes answers to the following questions: Why does the customer do business with us? Is the customer familiar with all of our products and services? What does it take for the customer to do additional business with us? What specifically does the customer like or dislike about our products and services? What specific changes would the customer make in our products or services? These and other questions—with drill-down in areas of special interest—form part of an intelligent approach to ensure that product and service design initiatives are never too distant from customer opinion and feedback.

The art form of survey design is easy to underestimate unless one has been at it for a while and experienced the many ways the process can go awry. Here are two examples:

1. I suffered a major and expensive gaffe in this area. We piloted a project to automate the lookup and assignment of commodity tariffs in the (at the time) all paper-based system of tariffs published by the Federal Maritime Commission. Our system was slick. An importer who wanted to bring, say, glass products into the country would enter *glass,* and the system would provide the most economical tariff designation by which to import glass into the country. Before we rolled the system out, we did the smart thing by hiring a respected consumer research firm out of the University of Pennsylvania to validate the market's acceptability of our product. A survey instrument was designed and administered to a sample of users in the shipping industry. Not unexpectedly, a very high proportion of respondents agreed that our system was indeed an efficient and cost-effective way to look up tariffs. We thought we had a winner. In the end, we spent $3 million to $4 million on a system that few would purchase. Why did this happen? Obviously, our survey design was flawed, but how?

   We thought we asked the right questions as to the expected efficiencies of the system, the price a customer would expect to pay, and so forth. What we never got around to asking was whether the respondent would in fact abandon the old system in preference to the new one. In other words, we had no way of gauging how strong the force of inertia was—the comfort in the old and the familiar—to continue the use of the manual system regardless of the advantages of the new automated system. Stated more simply, we never learned if the survey respondent met the conditions of being *ready, willing,* and *able* to purchase the new system.

2. Professor Clayton M. Christensen, in his book *The Innovator's Dilemma,* recounts how Eli Lilly and Company spent $1 billion in the 1980s to produce a human—not animal-based—insulin product that was 100 percent pure. The market's subsequent response, as Professor Christensen relates, turned out to be "tepid," as the company was unable to command a premium price for the product. The company had clearly overshot the needs of the market. How did this happen? Professor Christensen posits that the company perhaps listened too intently to leading endocrinologists whose practices focused on diabetes care.[14] This is a plausible explanation, but here is what it says about intelligent survey design: (1) a strong, influential, or leading customer's opinion cannot be allowed to drown out other customer voices when the enterprise is attempting to respond to mainstream market needs with new products; and (2) again, somewhere along the way, marketers, planners, and executives forgot to ask the customer if he was ready, willing, and able to purchase an apparently superior product.

The science in survey design involves the use of statistical methods to pretest, administer, and analyze survey results. Quantifiable survey data is useful only if it is statistically manipulated or if the sample and population sizes are very small as they might be in some business-to-business enterprises. How many customers do we need to sample in order to get results that reflect the entire population? What is the level of precision expected of the survey or delivered by the actual results? How confident do we want to be that the results are within our expected range of precision? Statistical measurement and analysis are beyond the scope of this book. Suffice it to say, however, that these techniques will allow us to infer if customer feedback, based on sample survey results, is representative of the whole population and thus the basis for product or service design decisions.

There are additional and important benefits to dialoguing with the customer in this way. To elicit feedback from the customer, to appreciate their expectations, to listen to their concerns; if we learned nothing about how to improve our offerings from these interactions, we would nonetheless be solidifying our relationship with customers simply by listening. Reaching out in a thoughtful, intelligent way is a very effective marketing tool as it signals to the customer how important he is to the supplier.

Finally, a customer survey properly designed and administered can serve as more than a pure research tool: it can be invaluable as a marketing and sales tool useful in disseminating information about a company's products and services. For example, a retailer conducting a survey might ask respondents if purchases made through their current retailer's online catalog can be returned to a store location in the customer's area. Deft design of the survey will leave no doubt in the respondent's mind that the surveying company clearly has the service in question. I have used this tool—that is, a combination sales pitch and research instrument—very cost effectively to reach a segment of the market that might have been unreachable by other means and at any cost.

The open-endedness of the customer information gathering process described above—asking questions, seeking feedback, listening, and dialoguing continuously with the different constituencies cited above will strike fear into the hearts of executives who seek a more orderly process. If it is calm and order that the executive seeks, then the process described above could not be further from that state of affairs. Calm and order is a metaphor which many executives—people in all walks of life, really—take as a signal that everything is just fine. The reality is, however, that too much calm and order can smell of decay. A product, a company, even a nation which achieves substantial stability has probably sounded its first toll of obsolescence.

Enlightened senior leaders who are committed to create the kind of environment where fresh and new ideas fuel the business in perhaps random and disruptive ways will have to resist the centripetal forces of the organization to restore its habitual equilibrium. Besides, the customer's voice in the Internet age is getting louder with each mouse click. Consumer experiences with lousy service, product flaws, and arrogant suppliers are now disseminated at broadband speeds for all to see. It is wise and courageous leadership who would rather shape trends than be victimized by them.

## BRING IN THE PLANNERS

The business planning function has two important roles to play in our quest for breakthrough customer-focused strategies. These are as follows:

1.  **The principal role is to** *provoke* **strategy—not to** *make* **strategy.** (If the planner is effective at making strategy, he should get out of the planning department as there is a more valuable role for him to play in the organization!). The planner's role is to *continuously*—I stress continuously because, again, the process has no beginning and, hopefully, no end—catalyze the organization to make strategy. The search for insights, as we have suggested, should reach out to organization insiders as well as outsiders, to company executives as well as the front line, to customers as well as prospects, and to competitors as well as partners. Remember, conventional marketing strategy is to push to the market the *next big thing*. The planner's role in our context is almost a polar opposite—that is, to ensure that new product and service initiatives are *pulled* by customer requirements so that the next big thing is less likely to be a product the market doesn't want, cannot use, or is unwilling to pay for. In this regard the planner has a number of important subroles:

    - To assist the organization's leadership by sourcing relevant industry and competitive trend data; validating such information for accuracy, completeness, and consistency; posing questions; and challenging assumptions.
    - To proactively seek out executives and frontline members of the organization who may have insights on ways to better serve the customer. This requires working in conjunction with marketing research specialists or other professionals designing surveys, questionnaires, and conducting focus groups to elicit intelligent feedback and opinions.
    - To reach outside of the organization to better understand expected customer requirements. Earlier we spoke of the need to find the customer's voice through intelligent survey design and administration. Dr. Seraku N. Kano, professor emeritus at the Tokyo University of Science, has developed acute insights for identifying customer needs. Professor Kano's model divides product or ser-

vice attributes along three dimensions: *must have,* which includes those attributes expected by the consumer and that therefore must be present in the product; *linear performance,* meaning attributes that impact the perception of the product in the consumer's eyes on a positive or negative scale; and *excitement,* which refers to attributes unexpected by the consumer and that can therefore result in high customer satisfaction.[15]

Whether a company chooses to work with the Kano model—other design techniques, such as quality function deployment (QFD) discussed later in this book, can work just as well—is not so much the point. The point is that the source for product and service design initiatives must originate from a customer need. Expert survey instrument design is required to elicit representative survey participant *behavior* and not just expressions of opinion. A survey respondent who extols the virtues of a product may or may not have the readiness, willingness, and ability to buy that same product (recall my gaffe with the tariff lookup system at the Federal Maritime Commission). Plumbing survey data for this distinction, as we have discussed, is crucial.

- To organize and classify the primal stew that results from numerous sources of information, feedback, and intelligence for review by executive leadership. Survey feedback data will inevitably prove to be conflicting and contradictory. That is the nature of the human factor at work. These contradictions must be resolved or understood to be irreconcilable survey data. The objective of this classification effort is to present survey insights in ways that might stimulate the development and articulation of new customer strategies. Again, this work might be undertaken jointly with the marketing research organization or outside research group.

2. **The secondary role is to *facilitate* the implementation of strategy.** Once a strategy or set of strategies has been identified, it is time to finally get analytical so as to select the best from the available strategic options. What are the tangible and intangible benefits of each strategic choice? How much is each strategy going to cost to implement? What is the approach to implementation? Do we have to engage in

pilots to test our assumptions? How do we prioritize the selected strategies? (We can't afford to implement every good strategic choice; some strategies may not be discretionary, and some that are may not be associated with hard dollar benefits). How many workers do we need to hire or fire as the case may be? How many facilities do we have to build or shutter? What will the impact of our new-found strategic choices be on our financial performance? How do we communicate this strategic initiative to the customer base or to our employees? And so on. Clearly, the work of implementation affects much of the organization, but the planner's role is pivotal in order to facilitate the effective execution of strategy.

## NO CUSTOMER, NO STRATEGY

A company doesn't have to know anything about its customers in order to project say, a 3 percent increase in revenues for the coming year—inflationary increases in the cost of living alone might account for the increase! Nor does it need much insight in order to respond to a competitor's initiative in the marketplace.

A customer-centric business-planning process must start by getting to know as much as is knowable about the customer. As a rule, the more insight a supplier has about the customer—and the more the supplier factors those insights into its business strategy—the more the supplier can respond to the customer's product and service needs. The upshot of seeking the customer's voice is that everybody wins. Conversely, drown the customer's voice, and the results can be devastating.

Here are some notable examples where the customer's voice was drowned out:

1. Prudential Insurance has made an art form of turning a deaf ear to the customer. In 1997 the company's securities brokerage unit paid expenses and fines totaling $1.5 billion levied by the California Insurance Commission for fraudulent sales practices that involved selling limited partnerships to investors, many of them elderly and with little savings, without explaining the attendant risks. In 1998 the company had to pay an estimated $2 billion to policyholders for inducing customers to cash in old policies and purchase new ones for

no apparent purpose but that it generated additional sales commissions for the sales agent. In 2006 the renamed, but not rehabilitated, securities brokerage unit of the company paid $600 million in fines, restitution, and penalties for *market timing*—surreptitiously trading more frequently than allowed by a mutual fund's prospectus—its mutual fund trades.[16]

2.  The subprime mortgage crisis, which began in 2007, racked up roughly $200 billion in defaulted mortgages as of October of that year. The crisis also violently convulsed the credit markets. Fannie Mae and Freddie Mac, government-sponsored enterprises chartered to provide a stable supply of mortgage money for home buyers, at last count, had sucked in $200 billion in order to remain solvent. The consequences of the crisis were so widespread that it could not spare many of the presumed titans of Wall Street: Bear Stearns, one of the largest underwriters of mortgage bonds, was bought by JPMorgan Chase for approximately seven cents on the dollar. Washington Mutual, the nation's largest savings and loan, was also bought by JPMorgan Chase, for approximately three cents on the dollar from its price a year before. Merrill Lynch was bought by Bank America in a shotgun wedding over a weekend (facilitated by much strong-arming by the federal government, the deal was approved by shareholders who were falsely told that Merrill Lynch executive bonuses of as much as $5.8 billion would not be paid without the bank's consent when in fact they had *already* been authorized).[17] AIG, the largest insurance carrier in the nation with much of its portfolio in mortgage-related products, had to be bailed out with a $160 billion loan by the federal government (the real culprit at AIG was a casino operation that sold insurance to hedge against exotic debt instruments). And Lehman Brothers, one of the most exposed banks to the subprime mortgage market, went out of business after 160 years!

Granted, home owners bore a great deal of the responsibility for the fiasco—lying about their incomes, living beyond their means, and so forth—but it is instructive to remember that mortgage brokers were incented to sell high-risk mortgages, and that mortgage underwriters processed applications without full documentation in order to handle ever-increasing volumes of loans. Lending institutions, for their part, securitized—that is packaged and sold off—these high-risk loans and thus shifted the risk to investors like you and me. The real estate bubble merely provided the tipping point for the crisis.

3. Telecommunications stock analyst Jack Grubman at Salomon Smith-Barney, with utter disregard for the investment public—never mind securities law—never was able to publish anything but the most unrealistically rosy outlooks on covered companies, bankrupt Worldcom being a notable example. Mr. Grubman also was at the center of a controversy when he raised his rating on AT&T stock from *neutral* to a *buy* ahead of that company's $10.6 billion issuance of stock at its wireless phone business. That piece of underwriting business was worth $63 million to Salomon Smith-Barney. The investment firm having pocketed those fees, Mr. Grubman proceeded to downgrade the stock again! In the end, Mr. Grubman was censured and permanently barred from the securities industry and forced to pay $15 million to settle charges against him.[18]

4. In the aftermath of the 2005 hurricane season, property and casualty insurers engaged in oftentimes deceptive practices to reduce risks, raise premiums, and lower claims payments. My insurance company, Chubb Insurance, raised the replacement value of my home by 32.5 percent with a commensurate increase in premiums in the first full policy year after the 2005 season. This was followed by a 10 percent increase in replacement value with a near 50 percent increase in premiums the following year. Keep in mind, these actions came in the face of the worst real estate market in the state of Florida in decades! I hired a well-known general contractor in the area to estimate the replacement value of my home and found the contractor's estimate to be less than *half* of Chubb Insurance's estimate. When the disparity was communicated to Chubb, I was informed, in so many words, to take it or leave it. I chose the latter. Allstate, the usual leader in customer complaints for home insurers with premiums in excess of $1 billion, dropped thousands of insured home owners in the state of Florida.[19] The company eventually saw its license to write policies suspended for its failure to cooperate with the state about its business practices. In an

August 2008 settlement with the state of Florida, the company agreed to lower home owner rates, write tens of thousands of new policies, and pay a fine of $5 million.[20]

Incidentally, these examples are hardly demonstrative of the free market economy at work. It must be pointed out that the federal government is very much complicit in the consumer rip-offs that continue to be perpetrated by the insurance industry by allowing these companies to compare costs in setting their rates. This collusion is unique to the insurance industry and permissible under the antitrust exemption provided by the McCarran-Ferguson Act of 1948.[21]

This section's heading, "No Customer, No Strategy," serves as both admonition and compass for action. The principal implications of which are as follows:

1. **New strategic initiatives, whatever else they might be, must be customer centric.** I know the CEO of a telecommunications broadband company who at an investor conference in New York justified plowing billions of dollars in capital expenditures to build network capacity. Incredibly, and with profound arrogance, this man announced that he was building this capacity because, as he said, "supply breeds demand." (Most of us would have been laughed out of our first course in economics if we had uttered this pap.) This same company has, since the CEO made his grandiose announcement, accumulated losses of more than $10 billion, while most of its buried fiber capacity remains dark. My memory may be slipping, but I don't believe there was any reference to customer needs or requirements in any of the CEO's grandiloquence.

   A plant manager wants to build a new plant? Fine. Now, how is that expected to benefit the customer? Improved labor productivity, improved capacity utilization, and so on, are not reasons per se to build a plant. Reduced product prices, improved failure rates—that is, enhanced product quality—if documented, are closer to the mark of our admonition. Here is a current favorite: a call-center manager wants to invest in additional equipment and people to reduce telephone queue—that is, wait—times. At first blush, this is a desirable objective. But how does this impact customer satisfaction? What is the customer reaction to current wait times? How many times does a customer hang up while waiting for an agent to answer the phone? Simply stated, if customer feedback does not allow us to *explicitly* make the connection between wait times and negative customer behavior, then the call-center expansion initiative has to drop down on the list of corporate priorities.

Here is one more example. The marketing department wants to install what is today the darling of the software world: customer relationship management (CRM) software. CRM is a very comprehensive suite of software that automates *customer-facing* corporate functions such as marketing, sales, and customer service. Implementation of this software is many times cited as emblematic of a company's customer focus—it must be the name! "We want to be totally customer-centric," is the reason given by an executive at a large chain of hotels for choosing to install CRM software. But, caveat emptor. This software is expensive to buy and maintain, and its installation can be quite disruptive to the customer base. On this last point, some companies merely cite a smooth installation as evidence of success! In the end, *success* can only be gauged on the basis of improved service to the customer. In the absence of customer service benefits, fittingly, both vendors and users have ratcheted down their expectations. Now the benefits are alleged to be improved sales-process automation, enhanced call-center efficiencies, cross-systems communications, and so on. These benefits, however notable, are incongruous with our admonition and therefore rank lowest on our priority scale of strategies.

2. **Customer-centric strategies must be anchored by the linch-pin of a qualified and well-supported front line free to operate in a culture of service**. New strategic initiatives cannot be implemented in an environment void of these conditions. Excellent troops cannot offset the disadvantage of working with mediocre armament. The reverse is just as true. Neither one of these conditions is conducive to substantive improvements in service. Nor, for that matter, is a strategy—no matter how unique and insightful—likely to lead to excellence in service in the absence of first-rate troops, well led and equipped with first-rate weapons. During the World War I, Winston Churchill, then first lord of the admiralty, was the

chief supporter of a scheme to force the Dardanelles—the sea-lane connecting the Mediterranean and the Black Sea. The scheme, in concept, was brilliant. Unfortunately, the Allies chose their commanders poorly for this operation, equipped the naval forces with obsolete vessels, landed inexperienced troops in insufficient numbers, and in the end, had no choice but to surrender the peninsula to the Turks. Thus was forfeited an opportunity to change the course of the War to End All Wars.

## IGNORING THE CUSTOMER IS FRAUGHT WITH PERIL

We conclude this chapter with another example—a far more personal example—of a customer's having lost his voice. The local phone company operating in Omaha, Nebraska, and surrounding states informed the public that it was about to embark on a program to lay broadband cable underground to allow it to deliver enhanced telecommunications services. As operators of a computer supercenter, serving domestic and international customers around the clock, our concern immediately turned to the possibility that a crew laying cable might accidentally cut power coming into our facility.

We contacted the company and were assured that their quality process was very detailed and sound, and that we should not expect any problems. You guessed it! Two days later, power was cut to the facility as well as to surrounding residential and commercial customers. Our backup electrical system, triggered by the outage from the public service, worked as expected, and power to the computer center was fed by emergency generators without interruption. Sporadically, and for several days that followed, public power to the computer center was interrupted. Despite our faith in the workings of the backup electrical system, our concern was that an overstressed component might succumb to a malfunction and bring the entire facility down. One day, I stopped to observe a cable-laying crew in action and finally understood the problem. I asked a man who was digging a trench, first in English, then in Spanish, if he could show me his site map indicating where it was safe to dig. He said he didn't have one, and that his boss, who had been on the job site earlier, had told him to dig in this location—as he pointed with his shovel. I had seen enough. I called the president of the phone company, but before I could finish making my point—namely, that he was going to kill my business—he said that I would have to talk to his assistant as he was running late to a golf tournament with Warren Buffet!

My next call went to our litigation attorney. That same afternoon, we went to court where we successfully argued before the judge that the phone company could not in the interest of delivering presumably enhanced services to its customer base, go about it as a bull in a china shop. The judge took all of 20 minutes to make his decision. We were granted a temporary restraining order. The phone company, henceforth, was barred from laying any more cable until it could demonstrate that it had a quality process in place.

In the year 2000, this former Baby Bell was purchased by Qwest Communications. Shortly thereafter, an executive vice president at Qwest commented, "We've lost more market share in Omaha than any other major market because we weren't focused on it." Further, the executive said, "Telephone companies used to be local, but we've been taking a mass-market approach."[22] No kidding!

# The Service Ethic

Empathy and trust are reflected not just in codes of ethics, but in organizational cultures that support ethical conduct.
—*Warren Bennis*
*On Becoming a Leader*

It was a beautiful day in June. The temperature was perfect, the sky was a bright blue, and there was a gentle breeze. My wife and I were scheduled to stay at the Aphrodite Astir Palace, a beautiful and romantic resort development surrounded on three sides by the aquamarine and placid waters of the Saronic Gulf, which laps the coast of Athens in Greece. Aphrodite—*Venus* in its Latin form—is the goddess of beauty and love. The goddess is often painted standing on a scallop shell or walking in the sea. The hotel, nestled in a wooded cove in the Vouliagmeni suburb of Athens, about 37 miles southeast of the capital, commands some of the highest room rates in all of Greece. Unfortunately, the quality of the service we experienced was commensurate with neither the stunning physical beauty of the hotel's setting nor its very lofty rates. In retrospect, I probably should have anticipated my eventual disappointment as I had to make numerous phone calls and send repeated faxes to simply receive confirmation of our stay and a car transfer from the airport.

As our car drove up to the hotel's front door, we were struck by the sartorial style of the porter: shirt unbuttoned to midchest, a cigarette dangling from his mouth. If we had not prodded him, our bags would still be in the car! Our suite was cramped, small, with broken hinges on furniture doors, and poorly equipped—no clothes iron, no minibar—albeit with a beautiful view of the sea from the balcony. The staff, to a person, was listless and incapable of exchanging a greeting with a guest. Yellow roses, which I had requested for my wife, were merely dumped on a table without the benefit of a vase and water. There was more. Repeated calls to housekeeping went unanswered. When I finally located a laundry valet, I asked her to press the wrinkles out of my suit in time for dinner. We never saw her again, and I never got my suit back until the following morning. Coffee delivered to the suite by room service was never served hot. I could go on, but you get the picture. It was obvious this so-called five-star resort was as overrated as it was overpriced.

After we checked out, a local businessman informed us that the hotel, as an affiliate of the Bank of Greece, was nothing more than another example of a government-run organization. The staff, he added, had simply been placed in their positions through the patronage of the government in power. That, I thought, was a simplistic explanation; government run or not, it is clear the staff at the Astir Palace is not imbued with an ethic of service. (This is a hugely ironic twist. In the Greek language, there is no word or expression for *customer service*. No insensitivity is implied by this omission. Walk into a restaurant, a department store, or hotel, and you will be asked, "How can we *serve* you?")

We had originally been scheduled to stay a minimum of two weeks at the hotel, but after just one day, we had seen enough. I called the manager to inform him that we were leaving and proceeded to the cashier to pay the bill. Not once was I asked if my stay, foreshortened by two weeks, had been satisfactory! Incidentally, hotel service in Greece can be superior. After our disappointment at the Astir Palace, we checked into the Athenaeum Intercontinental in Athens. There, accommodations were superb, and the service some of the best we have seen anywhere in the world.

## WHAT IS ETHICAL BEHAVIOR?

It was the early Greek thinkers who had much to say about ethical behavior. The Greeks had a lot to say about a lot of things, but theoretical speculation was their philosophical mainstay (to this day, the ubiquitous village Kafenion buzzes not only with local gossip but with the weighty issues of the day). Socrates, for example, suggested that wrongful actions are largely the result of ignorance, that is, of not knowing all of the facts. Plato thought that people desired to be good; the problem was knowing when and how to act.

If someone acted wrongly, it was because the person did not know right from wrong. Aristotle, Plato's student, went further and suggested that goodness was in the person and not the act itself. In other words, there is a distinction between *being* good and *doing* good. Plato's cardinal virtues of wisdom, temperance, justice, and courage were supplemented by Aristotle's own set of virtues and with a whole systematic way of looking at these virtues and, in the end, concluded that one should seek moderation—the middle ground or the *arithmetic mean* in Aristotle's words—in all things. Aristotle's approach to ethics, therefore, puts the individual's *character* front and center.

The Greek thinkers, profound as they were, remained theoretical in their discourse and thus did not lay down explicit rules in terms of right or wrong. The consideration of these rules is the province of practical or applied ethics. It was Immanuel Kant, perhaps the greatest philosopher of modern times, who pointed out that a moral imperative requires us to view our relationships with people in terms of a mutual interplay of rights and duties. In our business context, customers have *rights* to service, which is the *duty* of the service supplier. By extension, then, it is the *duty* of the customer to pay for the services received, which is a *right* of the supplier. These rights and duties, Kant said, are absolute. In other words, the rights of others must be respected regardless of conflicting interests. A right is an interest, which cannot be overridden without the consent of the person who possesses it. Likewise, duty is absolute. That is, a duty can only be satisfied when it has been fulfilled. Kant's approach to ethics, in contrast to Aristotle's approach, is that without rules the individual lacks the basis on which to make a correct ethical choice.

## ETHICS IN BUSINESS

"No employee may directly or indirectly offer or grant unjustified advantages to others in connection with business dealings, neither in monetary form nor as some other advantage"—so reads paragraph B.2 of German engineering giant Siemens AG's *Guidelines of Business Conduct*. Clearly, a lot of people at Siemens did not get the memo! According to a complaint filed by the U.S. Securities and Exchange Commission, between March 12, 2001, and September 30, 2007, Siemens made at least 4,283 payments totaling approximately $1.4 billion to bribe government officials, and an additional 1,185 payments totaling $391 million to bribe other third parties around the world. On December 15, 2008, it all came crashing down as Siemens agreed to pay more than $1.6 billion in fines in both the United States and Europe to settle the case.[1]

Ethics in business deals with the moral responsibilities and rights of individual employees. Business today appears to be far more cognizant of its ethical responsibilities than ever before. But as we see in the case of Siemens—and in the wake of Enron (accounting fraud), Tyco and Adelphia Communications (siphoning corporate funds for personal use), Wachovia (fraud on multiple levels), and former NASDAQ stock exchange chairman Bernard Madoff's $65 billion Ponzi scheme—it is clear that much work remains to be done. It should come as no surprise that the Ethics Resource Center in its National Business Ethics Survey of 2007 reports that during the year of their study, 56 percent of employees witnessed ethical misconduct of some kind.[2]

Most large organizations include rules of ethical conduct in their employee handbooks and provide employee training in ethics. Some organizations have established an office of ethics staffed with a senior officer, others operate hot lines to advise employees on possible conflicts of ethics or to anonymously report suspected infractions, and still others play board games as a training exercise.

Generally speaking, however, what passes for codes of ethical behavior are in fact codes of conduct. How is a code of ethics different from a code of conduct? The latter proscribes dishonest, illegal, or harmful acts. A code of conduct prohibits gambling, the use of alcohol or drugs, sexual harassment, the use of violence, and offering bribes. A code of conduct, therefore, more closely approximates a binary world of black and white. Such is not the case in the world of ethics framed as it is by fuzzy boundaries of behavior. No code of ethics can reasonably anticipate the ethical conflicts that can arise in the course of our interactions with customers, peers, bosses, and suppliers. For that reason alone, the most effective way to convey acceptable ethical behavior is by means of a concise statement of principles or imperatives backed up by solid enforcement guidelines.

I had a senior executive come to me one day with the news that he had found a request for proposal (RFP) response—a document normally containing the most sensitive and confidential information about a supplier—from a competitor that apparently had been left behind in a hotel conference room. The response represented an important piece of business for which we too were bidding, and so he asked me—perhaps wistfully—what he should do with it. I said, "Don't open it, and throw it away." He asked why. I was disappointed I was being asked the question in the first place, until I realized we had no reference point by which to guide this particular behavior. In the end, I was happy the executive asked the question, and we both agreed we had done the right thing.

Complex ethical dilemmas may prove troublesome without relevant points of reference. Stating prohibited behaviors—"it is unethical to lie," "it is unethical to misrepresent a fact," "it is unethical to make a commitment in the absence of the facts," and so on—is helpful, but keep in mind that a complete list of prohibitions is hardly possible. Some rabbinical scholars, by way of illustration, have enumerated 613 commandments in the Torah. Not all commandments are stated in the negative—"not to embarrass others," "not to oppress the weak," and so forth—but most follow the "thou shall not" formulation. Other scholars suggest there can be no end to such a list of commandments.[3]

Clearly, perspectives on ethics involve many aspects that can cloud a person's judgment. Emotions, depth of reasoning, absence of a single widely accepted ethical framework, access to facts, personal beliefs, and biases are among the many variables that can blur an individual's picture of what is right or wrong.

For example, it is conceivable that David Duncan, partner at the accounting firm of Arthur Andersen, took it upon himself to destroy documents—literally a mountain of documents—related to Enron's audits as a way to protect his client, a client he had served for seven years. Obviously, Mr. Duncan's loyalty—an otherwise honorable virtue—was manifestly perverse and thus hardly ethical.

Other complexities are in the offing. Key among these are the challenges that will attend a continually shrinking planet. As the world moves through ever-quickening stages of globalization, with potentially conflicting value systems among individuals, the stage is set for more and more complex ethical dilemmas to emerge. As Professor Samuel P. Huntington states in his provocative book *The Clash of Civilizations*, "Little or no evidence exists . . . to support the assumption that the emergence of global communications is producing significant convergence in attitudes and beliefs."[4] The opposite may be closer to the truth: a more globalized world may become a more conflicted world.

If a culture of honesty, integrity, and ethics is not the mainstay of the organization, then all of the articulated statements of improper behavior in the world are meaningless. In the end, we come back to Aristotle who believed that it is the individual's *character* that matters most and is thus the essential precondition to ethical conduct in business.

### REGULATION IS NOT A PROXY FOR ETHICAL BEHAVIOR

On July 30, 2002, President George W. Bush signed into law the Sarbanes-Oxley Act. President Bush said at the signing ceremony that the law constituted "the most far-reaching reforms of American business practices since the time of Franklin Delano Roosevelt."[5] In retrospect, President Bush should have reconsidered his reference to the Depression-era president whose centerpiece legislation at controlling business in the nation, the National Industrial Recovery Act (NIRA), was unanimously overturned in 1935 by the Supreme Court, which found the legislation overreaching by both the executive and legislative branches of government and therefore unconstitutional.

Sarbanes-Oxley, named after sponsors Senator Paul Sarbanes (D-MD) and Representative Michael G. Oxley (R-OH), is a U.S. federal law enacted in the wake of the Enron fraud to stem similar occurrences by instituting a number of regulations intended to attest to a firm's system of internal controls for the benefit of the investment public. Regardless of the official reason given for passing the legislation, I feel that this law was passed more by the need for Congress—spooked by Enron, to be sure—to prove to the public that they were on the job.

In the end, I don't believe that Sarbanes-Oxley is likely to ever prove to be cost-effective legislation, may actually impair a firm's competitive stance, and will likely not deter fraud long term. Here is why I feel the way I do:

- **The potential benefits of the law fail to offset the financial burden imposed upon companies.** The direct cost to business of complying with Section 404 of the act, the troublesome and costly provision requiring the actual attestation of the firm's internal controls, was estimated to have cost industry $15 billion to $20 billion when this was last studied in 2004. The indirect cost of applying Sarbanes-Oxley has received less study but is nonetheless very real as firms must now spend management time and resources to steer clear of potential litigation, while minimizing the cost of compliance. In a study by the RAND Corporation and the LRN-Center for Business Ethics, it was found that apart from compliance costs, the act imposes significant real costs on firms.[6] If that were not enough, the accountants-cum-regulators that make up the Public Company Accounting Oversight Board (PCAOB), created by Sarbanes-Oxley to regulate accountants and auditing standards, now run a bureaucracy of approximately $130 million per year as of the latest reporting year of 2007.

- **The accountants have become the new overlords in business**. At a time when we are losing our competitiveness in a world *not* governed by Sarbanes-Oxley, businesses risk being micromanaged by the accounting profession. Accountants now have to weigh in on management matters for which they are ill trained. Accounting is not an exact science; it is a profession based on judgment and flexibility. Yet, it is precisely judgment and flexibility that is proscribed by the law! Management for its part has become more bureaucratic and diffident, careful not to make a key decision that will raise the auditor's ire. As a leader, I want to act decisively: I don't want to stop, look, and listen to what the auditors have to say before I make an investment or operational decision that the management team and I feel strongly about making. There is no question but that the legislation raises the marginal cost of effecting organizational change that can only be borne by a consuming public.

- **Regulations cannot eliminate fraud.** Fraud can be mitigated by instituting company-specific checks and balances. Fraud cannot be eliminated, however, because the lock-pickers will always find a way. The acts of fraud and abuse perpetrated by company executives are the result of individuals operating in an ethical vacuum. All of the regulations in the world, therefore, will not prevent fraud. Remember, there were plenty of regulations in place at the time of Bernard Madoff's Ponzi scheme. The perpetrator was not apprehended before his confession, however, for the simple reason that the SEC bungled its own investigation and enforcement efforts.

    Similarly, there were regulations in place at the time of Enron's fraud. In that case, CFO Andrew Fastow *chose* to break the rules with his financial shell game. Enron's go-go culture is usually blamed for providing the spark for the massive fraud at the company, but even staid General Electric was guilty of cheating in 2002 and 2003 when it reported that it had sold 191 locomotives—all of them still in inventory—and by retroactively changing how it accounted for derivatives to avoid a $200 million pretax charge.[7] (Did you ever wonder how GE met analysts' earnings estimates so consistently?)

Additional regulations will not keep the *next* Madoff or Fastow from perpetrating a new set of chicaneries. A world without Madoffs or Fastows—a world perhaps chimerical—has a chance of succeeding only when ethical behavior is the pervasive culture in business. In the meantime, vigorous prosecution and severe punishment for offenders of existing regulations is probably better served than the passage of the next wave of regulatory prohibitions.

Let's face it: The only real winners from the Sarbanes-Oxley legislation are the public accountants. The Big Four—Ernst & Young, Deloitte, PricewaterhouseCoopers, and KPMG—are like pigs in mud, controlling 78 percent of all public company audits in the nation (representing 99 percent of public company revenues) and creating a concentrated market with huge cost inefficiencies. This oligopoly generated $90 billion in revenues and employed roughly 500,000 workers in 2007.[8] So much for looking after the investment public!

## THE SERVICE ETHIC IN ACTION

The service ethic refers to those principles and practices that govern how an individual and his organization behave toward the customer. The service ethic is not an offshoot of ethics in business or of ethical behavior generally. One can argue, quite convincingly, that there is just one ethical construct, which demands that we behave responsibly whether in or out of the world of business. Remember the Ten Commandments? The service ethic, however, is somewhat—but not entirely—confined by those interactions that take place between an organization and its customers but can also include the community at large. Our purpose here is to understand how the organization can better serve the customer by establishing the ethical foundations of those interactions. This understanding requires learning, practice, and reflection.

So how do we put the service ethic into practice? First, the organization needs to embrace a mission statement that places the customer at center stage (later in this chapter, we will have an opportunity to look more closely at a customer-focused mission statement as well as some counterexamples). A failure to place the customer at the top of the organization's priorities will be sure to create precisely the kind of ethical confusion that we are trying to avoid in the first place.

Second, putting the service ethic to work requires that the strategies, policies, procedures, and structures of the organization (1) do not subvert the mission and (2) are internally consistent. If crafting a mission statement is comparatively simple and straightforward, then ensuring that all enunciations of the mission are consistent throughout the organization represents truly hard work. For example, if the fine print in a credit application rejects a prospective buyer attracted by the local advertisement touting simply "no money down," not only is the organization's marketing undermined, but its ethical posture becomes suspect. Finally, I have always counseled that an individual's correct ethical choices should be grounded on the following two propositions, neither of which can be implied to bring harm to others:

- **Do what you say—or your organization says—you are going to do.**
- **Don't do what you say—or your organization says—you are *not* going to do.**

A firm adherence to these propositions speaks to the character of the individual and his organization. Can this organization be *trusted*? Is this an *honest* merchant? Does the company conduct business with *integrity*? These important moral and ethical qualities are in play each and every time a frontline worker makes a representation to a customer. And, a failure to abide by these propositions while making excuses or simply lying about why a stated promise wasn't kept gradually erodes the goodwill that has been built with the customer or keeps customer goodwill from being established in the first place.

An executive I know deals with a marketing representative of a computer company that she finds friendly and pleasant enough. She doesn't, however, trust anything he tells her because she's been lied to so many times. I am of the opinion that if this representative were replaced with a new face—as friendly and pleasant as his predecessor's—and if that new face told the truth forevermore, it would still take a very long time before the computer maker could count the executive as an important customer.

Admittedly more easily said than done, it is adherence to these propositions by everyone up and down the ranks, from the executive team to the frontline staff, that proves to be the single most effective way to prevent—and to recover from—lapses in service. Yet, this Golden Rule of service is more often than not a victim of corporate expediencies and rationalizations. Service mishaps, when they do occur, can usually be traced to nothing more complicated than a failure to abide by these rules.

These propositions can usually light a pathway of behavior for a whole range of day-to-day interactions with customers as well as with employees entrusted to serve them. Frontline workers who believe that senior management is not straight and fair with them cannot be expected to ignore their disaffection when dealing with customers; resentment will always betray the words or actions of disloyal employees to the detriment of the supplier. Ethical behavior, it can be said, begins in the executive suite.

Where the welfare of those with whom we interact comes face to face with ethical dilemmas, I come back to the two propositions above, supplemented by trust, honesty, integrity, and reference to similar past situations. In especially thorny circumstances, however, it is best not to act but to seek advice and counsel from peers, senior managers, or experts as appropriate.

## SERVICE IS A NON-ZERO-SUM GAME

The world of business is a rough-and-tumble enterprise among competitors. One side wins; the other side loses. (Even so, the role of a competitor, to paraphrase what U.S. Supreme Court Justice Louis Brandeis said almost a hundred years ago, is to best and not kill the competition.) That is as it should be if we believe that economic winners do a better job, over the long run, than losers in bringing to the marketplace superior, more cost-effective products and services. Economists and game theorists speak of such an outcome as being zero-sum: one participant's win is exactly offset by the other participant's loss. In a free market, of course, even losers win because they too are the beneficiaries of the availability of improved products and services.

A customer relationship, however, must be understood to be a non-zero-sum game. A classic win-win has both supplier and customer benefiting from each other's commercial interactions. This is a case where the sum of the interactions is *not* zero.

If competition describes the behavior that helps the enterprise acquire customers, then it is *cooperation* that allows the enterprise to retain customers. Cooperative behavior benefits the supplier in the conventional financial sense but in more subtle ways as well. A customer, particularly a cooperative one, is a beacon illuminating certain market needs and insights that the supplier might have no other way to acquire, except, of course, from another cooperative customer. Cooperative behavior, as it is symbiotic, also benefits the customer. How else, but with the supplier's cooperation, would the customer have the ability to fulfill his product and service needs; and in a business-to-business relationship, how else would the customer fend off *his* competition?

Cooperation between supplier and customer as well as between supplier partners opens new vistas that facilitate innovation and thus the creation of new wealth. This paradigm is simply not achievable except through the mutual cooperation of the participants. Cooperation creates a system of mutual and collective intelligence clearly superior to one that might exist if the parties were strictly transactional—not to speak of participants who viewed their relationship as one of tit for tat. Even nominal competitors can, at times, benefit more from cooperation than from competition. Unfortunately, the behavioral approach to business today is not to be generous but to resist giving what you are not *forced* to give. Examples abound.

I was averaging about 1,000 minutes per month with Verizon's wireless service, for over two years, when I realized that I had originally contracted for a monthly plan calling for 4,000 minutes. No amount of pleading with the provider led to any sort of an accommodation; they had me! Think how different my impression of this provider might be if they had taken the initiative to say, "Mr. Pupo, we notice you are using only a fraction of the plan you are paying for. Would you like to change your plan?" (I wonder if Lowell McAdam, president and CEO of Verizon Wireless, was thinking along the same lines when he said in his cover letter to his company's code of conduct that "integrity goes beyond laws and policies to also include the *spirit* [italics mine] of doing the right thing"?)[9] This should not have been a case of caveat emptor, but sadly it was.

On a more mundane level is the case of the local chain of Asian restaurants that uses imitation crab—basically a fish paste made with egg whites and tapioca formed to look like crab legs—in its seafood spring rolls. The menu, quite deceptively, clearly states the spring rolls are filled with *crab*.

The service ethic is the catalyst that provides a common ground, a common language even, on which cooperative behavior can exist between supplier and customer based on the core values of truth telling, flexibility, fairness, common goals, and reciprocity. The service ethic is the arbiter that ensures that service remains a non-zero-sum game.

One more example of what I mean will make the point. Our company offered to develop an electronic medical record (EMR) and system for patients of the big five hospitals operating in Omaha, Nebraska. An EMR, very simply put, is a digital record of all that transpires in the medical history and care of a patient. In the vast majority of cases, the patient's medical record is archived by a clinic or hospital as a file folder containing mostly paper forms and notes as well as radiological images. Needless to say, the paper-based medical record is an administrative nightmare that creates huge inefficiencies in storage and retrieval with risk of loss or destruction of vital documents.

The system our company proposed carried a tab of $10 million, of which we offered to put up half. Each hospital, therefore, needed to come up with $1 million. A number of financing schemes were available to help each hospital fund their proportionate share, and it was clear that system efficiencies would help recover the hospital's investment. When it was all said and done, one hospital CEO strongly supported the effort, two were on the fence, and two were opposed. Physicians argued mostly about which group of doctors would have the biggest say in influencing the design of the system. The two institutions opposing the system were also the strongest financially and thus felt no great need to collaborate with their competitors even though installation of the system could not possibly have changed an institution's market share. Unfortunately, the project could not go forward without the two opposing institutions. The project died, never to be resurrected. Lost in the competitive whirlwind, most regrettably, was the opportunity to help the community with an improvement in the service and cost of its health care experience.

## CUSTOMERS ARE FIRST

Articulating a mission is a most important step in focusing the organization's priorities and principles. We made reference in chapter 1 to our company's mission statement and how it makes no bones about where our priorities lie. The mission is brief, so I'll repeat here in full:

- **Customers are first—We will provide service to ensure the highest level of customer satisfaction.**
- **Quality—To achieve customer satisfaction, the quality of our work must meet the highest standards, those of our customers.**
- **Business partnership—By developing a partnership with our customers, we share in the responsibility for satisfying their business objectives.**
- **Ethics—We will conduct business in an ethical, legal, and socially responsible fashion. Our integrity will never be compromised.**

It is a validation of an organization's commitment to a customer focus that there be widespread agreement and support for a core set of beliefs such as these. Intellectually, and emotionally, members of the organization must agree to perform according to what is essentially a compact with their customers. Why are there just four statements of principle—not five or six or some other number—in the mission statement? Are the principles stated in rank order? Why doesn't the mission statement mention shareholders or employees? What about the organization's obvious need to make a profit? Differences of opinion, disagreements, and alternate views can be debated, but at the end of the day, everyone must close ranks on the agreed-upon set of values. If not, senior leadership needs to respond decisively. Training sessions, seminars, formal meetings, and ad hoc gatherings all provide an opportunity for the leadership to drive home the organization's values.

It is a sobering thought, however, that no matter the lengths to which the leadership goes to inculcate the employee population in the organization's fundamental values, it will frequently have to deal with either lapses in performance or, more egregiously, in commitment. My experience has taught me that while the former can be addressed effectively with additional training, the latter has no possible remedial outcome.

There is no question but that a strong conviction in the core beliefs, individually and collectively, of the mission statement above provides the *basis* for a customer focus to drive the business. As we said earlier, however, it is adherence to the service ethic that ensures that a customer focus is long lasting and sustainable.

I am often struck, as I reread the mission, not only by the timelessness of the message but by how effectively and succinctly it speaks to what our company is all about. Incidentally, the company's mission is hard to ignore. The mission statement is printed in employee handbooks and laminated, wallet-sized cards; it is prominently displayed in the boardroom, in the office, on cubicle walls, on desktops, in entrance lobbies, on the company's Web site, and in marketing brochures.

Jeffrey Abrahams has written a most useful book entitled *101 Mission Statements*.[10] Any company considering crafting a mission should consult Mr. Abraham's book. I note with interest, however, that of the 101 missions stated in the book, only 9 clearly acknowledge their commitment to the customer in their opening statements. Some missions are mystifying (Radioshack Corporation: "Radioshack's mission is to demystify technology in every neighborhood in America"); some missions are not mission statements at all (Adobe Systems Corporation: "Adobe revolutionizes how the world engages with ideas and information"; or Dreyer's Grand Ice Cream Holdings: "To become the pre-eminent ice cream company in the United States"); and others leave you wondering (Armstrong World Industries: "Simpler, Faster, Better, Together"). Still others let you know where the customer stands. First Horizon National Corporation has six core values. Of these, employees rank first in line, the customer fifth! When you consider that Mr. Abrahams culled the best of the best of the available mission statements, you begin to appreciate the uphill battle we have in putting the customer first.

The service ethic cannot be bought with dollars. That is encouraging to some, not so to others. It is encouraging to the entrepreneurial company—regardless of size, industry, or amount of time in business—whose leadership and culture is adaptable to the rapidly changing mores of our time. It is more distressing, however, to the enterprise that, although endowed with deep pockets, is saddled by a legacy that militates against cultural change. That is too bad. Arnold Toynbee, the great historian, said that civilizations die from suicide and not other causes. The same might be said of corporate cultures.

## QUALITY AS AN ETHICAL STANDARD

In my neighborhood, there is a photo-lab that prominently advertises a one-hour processing service. I take lots of pictures, and so I get to visit this lab frequently. My experience has been that of the many times I have requested one-hour service, I have never been asked to return within the hour. On the contrary, I'm always reminded how busy they are and could I please return in two to three hours!

For the most part, *quality* remains a misunderstood term. Academics, especially, who seek to define terms that fit comfortably in compartments—a taxonomy, the scholars would say—continue to struggle to define the term. When they do, no two definitions are consistent. Our approach, less scholarly perhaps, consists of common sense and intuition; it consists of listening to the customer.

After World War II, pioneers in the field such as W. Edwards Deming, Philip Crosby, and Joseph Juran hammered home the message—an important message, to be sure—that quality was a response to a specification. As a result, quality as an output of the production process had to be measured against a predetermined benchmark. This call was then taken up by standards bodies such as the International Organization for Standardization (commonly referred to as the ISO), which continue to stress a definition of quality that is profoundly circular: an organization establishes a set of requirements or specifications for a product or service, which, if adhered to in the production of said product or service, meets a quality standard. It is hard to argue with that logic! In other words, if our quality standard for the underwriting of loans is 95 percent, then so long as we maintain a 5 percent defect rate, we are within our standard for quality. Again, we have an irrefutable, albeit unhelpful, set of facts. In fairness, there is nothing in the work of experts in the field of quality that would have the organization rest on its laurels and be satisfied with a given defect rate. On the contrary, the message is always to continually improve the process. It is that part of the message, however, that for the most part falls on deaf ears.

Quantitative measurement and repeatable processes dominate the quality certification criteria to this day. As long as some stipulated set of measures is satisfied, the theory goes, quality is presumed to exist, and yet there is no evidence correlating quality with certification. Meanwhile, there is as much quality production coming from uncertified suppliers as from those who are certified. But the larger question has got to be: what does certification say about whether the supplier satisfies the intended use or purpose of the product or service? Unfortunately, service-level specifications alone are not enough to deliver superior quality. Excellence may not be repeatable every time, even if the processes are repeatable, because the focus is efficiency and not responsiveness to the needs of the market. The classic definition of quality, which only recently has begun to change, leaves little or no room for imagination, inspiration, improvement, or responsiveness to the needs of the market. It is a definition with no degrees of freedom. It is fixed, objective; its outcome, statistical.

There is another way to look at quality. It simply requires taking the customer's point of view. This definition is far more saturated with subjective interpretation and therefore proves more difficult to deal with. But deal with it we must. To achieve customer satisfaction, the quality of our work must meet the highest standards, not those of a standards body, or of our own making, but of our customers. This view is not universally held. Even Edwards Deming, who understood that the consumer was the most important part of the "production process," states in his classic work, *Out of the Crisis*, that "quality *should* (italics mine) be aimed at the needs of the consumer present and future." I hardly find this a ringing endorsement of the role of the customer to whom quality *must* always be aimed.[11]

A supplier who satisfies his own supplier-stipulated defect rate is clearly satisfying a standard for quality, the definition of which only the supplier controls. So what's the point? Customer expectations, fluid as they are, constitute a potentially ever-changing standard of performance. Supplier performance measured in the absence of known customer expectations is futile. In their classic studies on service quality, authors L. L. Berry, A. Parasuraman, and V. A. Zeithaml determined that there are five factors impinging on the customer's perception of service quality.[12] These factors are as follows:

1. **Reliability (the ability to provide what was promised)**
2. **Responsiveness (the willingness to help customers promptly)**
3. **Assurance (the knowledge and courtesy of employees)**
4. **Empathy (the degree of caring and of individual attention)**
5. **Tangibles (the physical appearance of facilities, equipment, etc.)**

I mention the work of these authors because subsequent research on the authors' studies found that there is nearly an inverse relationship between the factors that matter most to customers and those factors that suppliers perform best. Reliability, for example, is the single most important factor that shapes customers' perceptions of service quality. Yet, reliability is perceived by customers as the weakest factor of supplier performance. Tangibles, the least important factor to customers, is believed by customers to be the area best handled by suppliers! The same evidence was found in J. D. Power and Associates' *North American Airline Satisfaction Study of 2008*. In that study, passenger dissatisfaction with the airlines was more often due to discourteous crew members than to factors such as the quality of the craft, reservation procedures, or pricing.[13]

Dr. Yoji Akao and Dr. Shigeru Mizuno designed a product development methodology in the late 1960s called quality function deployment (QFD), which was meant to allow planners to get product and service design closer to the customer.[14] This approach to quality has a customer orientation that other approaches lack, focusing as it does on having a full grasp of the customer's needs and expectations as a precursor to downstream product development activities. The objective of the approach is to ensure that the end product is faithful to customer and market needs as a way to enhance customer satisfaction. The process methodology is intense in its information and documentation requirements. It calls on senior leadership to stay focused on understanding the expressed quality needs of the customer when the prevailing product design culture would much rather be reliant on past experience and intuition.

What role, then, does quality play in our construct of the service ethic? My benchmark is as follows: Quality is believed to be *implicit* in all products and services—for example, a new software release is understood to abide its technical specifications and to be free of known bugs—and as such must be provided by the supplier. (It is instructive to note that the Japanese use an analogous term, *atarimae hinshitsu*, to mean that a product works as intended.) To my way of thinking, the omission of implicit quality—or to represent that it is present when in fact it isn't, or to downplay its importance, and so forth—is clearly inimical to the service ethic.

Thorny issues remain. Who is to say whether a product attribute is implicit or not? There are no hard-and-fast rules here, only the supplier's forthrightness in conveying its product attributes to the marketplace. Is electrostatic discharge protection implicit in the quality of consumer electronics? What about side curtain air bags in SUVs? Each of these is in the state of the art of their respective industries, yet each has been slow to emerge. Can a supplier *knowingly* suppress a quality attribute—due to cost or other considerations—which it believes, or is led to believe, to be implicit in a product or service? The answer is yes, provided there is an explicit disclosure of the attendant inconveniences, and perhaps hazards, of such omission, and until, of course, any of these attributes become legally mandated. In the end, the customer-focused supplier follows the dictates of the market.

## SERVICE: QUALITY VERSUS QUANTITY

A fundamental belief of the service ethic is to provide the same quality of service to all customers. Putting this belief into practice requires adherence to a process that does not make a distinction for large versus small customers, affiliated versus nonaffiliated customers, high-margin versus low-margin customers, and so forth. In translating the strategies and beliefs in this book into day-to-day practices, it is the service *quantity*—offering a discount for volume purchases or cash payment is in keeping with our rule, but not bumping a passenger, with a reservation, from a flight in favor of a frequent flier—that necessarily varies by customer, and not the *quality*. To do otherwise is to engage in a form of *redlining*, and that practice is clearly not ethically sustainable in any context.

A software development company we had a hand in starting up in Mexico made a crucial mistake in this area. In a joint business development effort, we helped this company to become one of the earliest software development centers south of the border. The company was staffed by young, educated, and quite precocious men and women as programmers. It was our plan to provide software programming resources out of this center to one of our large South American customers. The center was a big success. It was featured in the local press and was even visited by President Ernesto Zedillo who cut a dashing figure in his brown leather jacket surrounded by a sizeable security detail. The president gave a rousing speech and sang the praises of a new era in Mexico.

The software company, after our project was on its way, was awarded a similar, though much larger, project by General Electric. It was indeed a prestigious win for the software company. The problem arose when the management of the company, so intent on impressing GE, cannibalized the best people they had assigned to our work. Quality dropped significantly, and customer complaints rose dramatically. In the end, we had no choice but to cancel the contract with the software company. Of course, we never used this company again.

## CUSTOMERS AS PARTNERS

To take a narrow or opportunistic, largely financial or transactional, view of a partnership is to almost guarantee its short duration. An alternative view of a partnership requires patience, maturity, vision, and good faith. Relationships are seeded with the potential for either of these views to prevail. The onus is on the supplier, however, to explore whether reciprocal good-faith action can be expected from the customer that will give long life to a relationship. I'll relate a couple of examples from my international experience to make the point.

Our company had been negotiating for months to form a software development joint venture in Bangalore, India, as a way to supplement our development capacity in the Americas and in Europe. Our prospective partner was chairman and CEO of a very successful private company with a variety of businesses far-flung throughout India, Malaysia, Singapore, and Indonesia. We were keen on making this relationship work and accordingly had agreed to most demands, but one stumbling block, having to do with voting control, kept getting in the way. It looked to us like the deal would crater.

At a particularly heated juncture during the negotiations, the chairman cast aside the vehement objections of his advisors that might further have stalled, if not altogether killed, the deal. Understanding the genuineness of our position, the chairman indicated to his negotiating team that he could live with the arrangement as proposed, and that besides, "It was God's will that our companies come together." All objections thereby resolved, the negotiations moved forward to a successful conclusion. Metaphysics aside, the chairman's actions demonstrated visionary leadership as the venture stood the test of time.

Here's a somewhat different story with a decidedly different ending. Our company, working in conjunction with a Big Four accounting firm, was asked to develop a plan to rationalize the computing and related administrative costs of the Dutch and German

subsidiaries of a metal packaging company. The Dutch computing facilities were poorly equipped, ineffective, and not very well
staffed. Literally 200 miles distant, across the border into Germany,
was a sophisticated mainframe computing facility that with a modest investment for increased capacity could serve the needs of both
companies. The center was staffed by top-notch technicians, managers, and administrative professionals. The redundant facilities
and staff were costing the parent company millions of dollars a
year. The recommendation was clear: shutter the Dutch operation,
and service computer users in both countries from the upgraded
German center.

The upshot of the recommended plan was that both service and
cost would be dramatically improved for each of the subsidiaries.
Furthermore, many affected Dutch employees would be offered
positions in the new computer center. It seemed like a partnership
made in heaven. It was not to be. Workers, union leaders, and poli-
ticians, always sensitive—subtly but persistently—to the memory
of the six-day German blitzkrieg of 55 years before, defeated the
plan before it could see the light of day. Redundant facilities and
staff were left in place, millions of dollars continued to be spent,
and poor service to computer users in Holland persisted. So much
for partnership!

As a supplier partner, I want to know as much about the customer's business as the customer is willing to tell. I don't want to
know anything I shouldn't know, but the more I know, the more
I can help. Generally speaking, the more the supplier knows about
his customer, the more the supplier can become an active and con-
tributing member to the customer organization. Don Peppers and
Martha Rogers refer to this type of relationship with customers as
*collaborative marketing.* Peppers and Rogers, in their fine book *The
One to One Future,* describe at length how a supplier can use information elicited from each customer to promote a collaborative relationship: "The more individual, customer-specific data you have,
the more capable your firm will be when it comes to creating collaborative opportunities with your customers."[15] This will allow the
supplier to more closely tailor products and services to meet the
customer's needs, volunteer solutions, and preempt problems before arising—that is, to work in partnership. Not every customer,
however, seeks this kind of relationship.

A CEO I know leads a small, albeit very creative, software company. One day he was having a meeting with the vice president of

information technology of a multibillion-dollar health care provider early in their relationship. The vice president opened the meeting by reciting in a rapid-fire manner the extensions he wanted to see in the next version of the software. My friend, the CEO, wanted to learn more details about the need for such changes and asked the vice president to be very specific about his requirements. The CEO, sensing annoyance on the part of the vice president, offered that as partners on this project it was important for him to document everything with great accuracy. At this, the vice president barked that he wasn't looking for a partner; he was looking for someone to do as instructed!

That this executive was not looking for a partner is evident from what is known in an unrelated case. In that case, another small software provider filed suit to recover $500,000 for nonpayment of licenses used by the corporate giant. The suit alleges that the software company was instructed to install the software, which it did, in anticipation of a purchase order that never came. The health care company, for its part, claims the installation was not properly authorized. The case is still pending.

If we believe that a relationship will not mature past the formalism of the written contract, then the kind of synergy that can spring from the members of the participating organizations will never materialize, to the detriment of all. So what do we look for in a thriving partnership? An abundance of integrity and trust, and the absence of win-lose games. Chip Bell, who as author, consultant, and educator has done more than anybody I know to elevate the status of the customer as partner, believes a customer partnership is comprised of six qualities: generosity (which Bell calls abundance), trust, dreams, truth, balance, and grace.[16] This list of qualities, arguably not an exhaustive list of all of the necessary qualities needed for a successful partnership, is striking as it speaks exclusively to the *ethical* posture of the participants as playing the key role in a healthy business relationship. Partnerships are reciprocal obligations: customers and suppliers must meet halfway. Without reciprocity, there is no foundational basis for a healthy relationship.

Here is an example of what I mean. In November 2005, one of the largest building materials companies in the United States invited our company, after 10 years of service, to participate in a competition with 22 other providers for their logistics business. There had been a management change with our customer executive point of contact, so we had a mild concern that the relationship might undergo some changes, but in the end, we felt our service, always unimpeachable, would carry the day. In February 2006, we were informed we had bested the competition and signed a three-year agreement. This was a very large win for our company, and we felt very good about having come out on top of such a large field. Shortly after the deal was signed, we sensed a noticeable difference in the quality of our communication. Meetings became more infrequent. Telephone conference calls were very matter of fact. The relationship had become very transactional. In the aftermath, it all became clear.

Nine months later, we were notified that the customer was taking its business elsewhere. That was their decision, despite the fact that we surpassed every service level agreement (SLA) condition, such as on-time deliveries and inventory accuracy. Moreover, the quick exit would cost the customer dearly in order to bulk-transfer huge amounts of inventory as soon as possible. No matter. This customer wanted out. Repeated calls to the new executives in charge went unreturned. The CEO, to whom I appealed via e-mails, overnight letters, and telephone calls—not so much to have the contract reinstated, but to learn and understand the *why* behind their actions—never had the common courtesy to engage. Clearly, we were prepared to meet whatever reasonable condition this very important and long-term customer might have in mind. After working together for so long, we thought we owed it to the relationship.

What possible ethical justification did our former customer have for the actions it had taken? This company—the very same company with a code of conduct that prohibits employees from accepting lunch and dinners from suppliers—could never muster the courage to sit down with us and say, "Look, we know you've been our supplier for over 10 years, but this is why we are leaving." It was not to be. The epilogue to this story is that as soon as the last truck was out of our facility, the company that our customer had chosen as their new provider became involved in a stockholder revolt, an employee insurrection, and a boardroom action that saw the CEO sacked after he faced allegations of embezzlement.

## A PARTNERSHIP CAN BE SABOTAGED BY LEGALISMS

Our company worked with a lender for a number of years until a management shake-up left our account in the hands of a young banker who was very full of himself. When it came time to renegotiate our agreement, we sat down and hammered out a set of principles around which contract language could be drafted. When we received final documents, however, we were shocked. The agreement had morphed into something altogether different: the banker's proposed contract bore no resemblance to our term sheet, and extraneous provisions generous to the lender were included where none existed before. Repeated attempts to bring the negotiation back to the original terms were for naught. Weeks and months passed, meanwhile our legal expenses zoomed and tempers flared.

Now, I admit that lending money is a risky business, and that a lender needs to be circumspect about its lending practices. (In truth, Shylock's cruel behavior in Shakespeare's play *The Merchant of Venice* has become a powerful if unfortunate parable of the moneylender's trade that generations of bankers have found difficult to shake.) So too are changes to be expected as a term sheet transitions into a final document. Such is the nature of the process of drafting contracts. But I found moving the goal posts to the 50-yard line *after* an agreement in principle had been reached contemptible.

The banker's behavior, rationalized often as, "We have to protect our interests," is a perfect example of what Robert Solomon, a professor of philosophy, calls *abstract greed*. That is, greed without a specific purpose. As Professor Solomon puts it, abstract greed is "a set of myths that allows and encourages the vices to be paraded as virtues, selfishness to overwhelm mutual goals and fellow feeling, mutually destructive competition to win over cooperation and real efficiency."[17] After great expense and much time wasted, we took our business elsewhere.

The fundamental purpose of a customer focus is to nurture and preserve customer relationships for the long term. This purpose has its roots in a very basic assumption: every customer we have is forever. Obviously, we can't live with this assumption unless we think of long-term customer relationships as being unbounded by contract provisions, timelines, or other formalities.

There are two faces to a customer-supplier relationship. The first has to do with the formal, explicit relationship between the parties; the second, with the largely undefined relationships that organically grow between and among individuals. The sustainability of successful relationships lies not in their ability to abide the explicit contractual obligations of the parties but to *transcend* such obligations.

Partnering, in this context, is an act of developing kinship in order to nurture commitment and cultivate loyalty. This is the kind of relationship where many of the rules of engagement are largely unwritten as they are heavily dependent on the interpersonal instincts or relationships of the parties.

Businesses engaged in complex service creation and delivery are challenged to codify contract terms with precision. Computer service contracts, an area that I'm very familiar with, are notorious for the difficulty they pose in defining with precision the rights and responsibilities of the parties. On the other hand, many in the legal profession continue an age-old practice of attempting to show their worth by the girth of the contract documents they churn out.

The simple fact is, more times than not, we can't think of all the possible ways in which customer and supplier might have to work together—the possibilities are endless over the life of a contract. Perversely, once a certain point is reached—an admittedly difficult point to identify—in codifying the responsibilities of the parties, any further attempts quickly reach a point of diminishing returns. In this respect, overdoing contract language gives rise to the situation we have with the federal income tax code where additional provisions dreamed up to close loopholes actually *increase* them and the swirl of controversy that surrounds them. It is little wonder that the code now runs to over 16,000 pages and counting!

It is emblematic of a healthy relationship between the parties that the members of the participating organizations behave with considerable flexibility. The greater burden of such flexibility, however, lies with the supplier. So, when the customer says, "I need 'A'," the supplier will recognize that the customer needs help and will not be driven to fetch the contract and reply, "Well, Mr. Customer, 'A' is not in the contract." Instead, the focus will be on satisfying the customer's need, for what matters is this: "A" is a problem for the customer, and we need to figure out how to deal with it. This approach, I have found, is anathema to many attorneys who in their zeal to serve their client—or their ego—will attempt to craft airtight agreements even at the risk of antagonizing the customer prospect and opposing counsel. In one case, I had no choice but to dismiss our counsel as he risked killing a deal for us with his constant pettifoggery.

Ultimately, clever deal making and legal pyrotechnics are poor substitutes for partners that see eye-to-eye on the merits of a relationship and collaborate fully to execute its mission.

## COMMUNICATION: A KEY WEAPON OF
## THE ETHICAL PROVIDER

No matter one's dedication to the espoused ethics of service, the limitations of natural language and its grammar contain the potential for discord when none is anticipated, let alone expected. The more complex the transaction the supplier is attempting to codify, the more likely it is subject to the vagaries of language. Vague and ambiguous communications can undercut an otherwise healthy relationship between customer and supplier.

*Vague* communications, whether written or oral, fail to provide distinct parameters for action. A device warranty representation will proclaim: "When the device fails, we will dispatch a technician to repair the problem." This warranty seems pretty straightforward until you start testing the boundaries of the representation. What exactly constitutes a *device failure*? Does a device failure mean that the device has no functionality whatsoever, or that it has partial functionality? What about sporadic failures? Under what conditions do any of these scenarios trigger the dispatch of a technician? How soon after a reported failure is a technician dispatched? Does *repair* include device replacement? And so on.

Precision in communication is the ethical supplier's best friend because it allows both the customer and the frontline staff a better chance to grasp whatever is being represented: "When the device fails to perform, in conformance to the attached specifications, a technician will be dispatched, within 24 hours of receipt of notice, to restore the device to its original specifications or replace it with the same or similar device of at least equal specifications." The time required to articulate such a representation is well worth the effort as misunderstandings or worse—the potential of which can never be eliminated given the inherent limitations of natural language—will be kept to a minimum.

Imprecision—assuming it isn't deliberate in an attempt to obfuscate—can undermine a supplier's otherwise fine work and reputation because the rhetoric might not correspond with the intended actions. A supplier who means to stand by the second warranty representation above but whose formulation is more like the first unwittingly invites misunderstandings, arguments, and ill will.

*Ambiguous* communication takes place when a term, word, or phrase can be interpreted in more than one way. Using the word *biweekly* in a contract is a good way to start an argument between supplier and customer where in its place either *twice a week,* or *every other week,* conveys the intended meaning.

Here is a representation exploding with ambiguity: "Supplier warrants that the faulty device will be restored to good working order." Does *restore* mean repair or replace? Does *good working order* refer to the original performance specifications of the device? Or, will the device be restored so that it is simply functional?

Ambiguity is the sandbox of the poet ("All the earth grows fire, White lips of desire")[18] but the minefield of the business person. Precision in written or oral form is the best antidote to combat ambiguous and vague communications. And, in the case of the ethical supplier who has nothing to hide by being imprecise, there is much to lose from lazy, sloppy messaging. In 1999 the Metropolitan Life Insurance Company settled a class action lawsuit at a cost of $1.7 billion for sales practices, which among other things, represented life insurance policies as *retirement vehicles* whose premiums would end after some stipulated period of time. That time never came, and policyholders had to come up with additional cash or lose their policies.[19]

We may come to a point where despite the best efforts on the part of the supplier to communicate clearly, there still results a difference of opinion on the interpretation of some representation contained in a sales document, warranty, or contract. In this case, customer and supplier each believes his interpretation is *not* ambiguous but that each has it right. What to do? Stop providing further service to the customer? That might constitute a breach. File a lawsuit? Kiss that customer goodbye! None of the available options that involve drawing a line in the sand stands a chance at maintaining customer goodwill.

In criminal jurisprudence, ambiguity triggers the rule of *lenity.* This is a rule that, although not applied uniformly, requires that ambiguities in the law be resolved in favor of the defendant. In a similar vein, the ethical supplier, having exhausted all of his arguments aimed at disproving the existence of an ambiguity—that is, at trying to prove the merits of his position—is advised, in the end, to cede to the customer's interpretation or seek some fallback compromise position (and rewrite the nettlesome provision at first opportunity!). This is potentially strong medicine, depending on the scope and scale of the concession, and I am not suggesting this action be taken lightly. I am suggesting, however, that such a course of action can not only inform the supplier on the importance of clarity in communications but can also defuse a potentially damaging dispute with the customer. Further, a goodwill gesture such as this will hardly be lost on the customer.

Let me relate an example of what I mean. An equipment distributor of our choosing once installed a piece of communication gear on the premises of a customer, a financial services firm, which allowed it to connect the customer's sales staff to a computer system application that we operated remotely. Shortly after installation, the equipment would sporadically black out, thereby shutting down all communications to the customer's computer system. For all intents and purposes, our customer could not conduct any business during these outages. The problem proved intractable to engineers for weeks. Thirty days later, a microcode bug—a manufacturer's defect—was found and removed, and service returned to normal.

We were embarrassed and tried to understand from a reading of the contract what our obligations—our legal liability—might be. I personally thought that our representations in this area were ambiguous. Our lawyers felt that the distributor was at fault—or following the chain of liability, the manufacturer—and that the liability was rightly placed with the distributor. The customer's point was that but for our selection and recommendation of the chosen distributor, he would not have experienced the outages. Further, the customer claimed we should have exercised greater quality assurance over the installation procedures undertaken by the distributor's technicians.

Our vice president of technology and I flew to St. Paul, Minnesota, where our customer was located. We got to the point quickly. We apologized for the service interruptions and took full responsibility for the problem. In so doing, we ignored our own lawyers' advice. We then proceeded to forgive our entire service fees for the month in question. The moral obligation we felt was huge and palpable. In the end, this customer reciprocated with years of loyal business and was one of our most enthusiastic references.

Practically every contract or other language dispute I have been involved with has turned on the supplier's—or supplier's counsel's—failure to properly define terms in the agreement. What exactly is meant by *modular integration* or *upward compatibility*? How about *defect rate*? These terms have all been the source of debate between supplier and customer. I have also found, however, that every disagreement has planted within it the seed of a customer experience that can not only nullify the negative occurrence but can linger in the customer's mind for its *positive* character.

## CUSTOMERS FROM HELL!

"Customers from hell" is how one participant in Ron Zemke and Kristin Anderson's focus group described their most difficult customers. The picture that emerged from the focus group interviews, according to Zemke and Anderson, was not pretty: "We heard about customers who belittle, demand, threaten to get physical, *get* physical, throw tantrums, throw heavy objects, spew poisonous invectives, lie, rant, and, in general behave like Caligula on a bad day."[20]

Unfortunately, despite our best attempts to seek out customer relationships that can mature into true partnerships, the reality is that there will be times when a supplier may discover that it has made a serious mistake in its choice of customer-partner. (Actually, customers from hell show their horns very early in the relationship.) Aggressive and hostile behavior on the part of individuals can have myriad causes: fear, stress, anxieties, frustrations, doubts, and confusion all can lead to unpleasant exchanges between people. In the world of business these behaviors come with the territory and we shouldn't expect anything to change anytime soon. Customers from hell, however, seem to take their aggression to a different level. When things are not going their way these individuals are not beyond turning to confrontation or even bullying their suppliers.

One of the most hostile customers I ever encountered suffered a severe case of buyer's remorse as he was instructed by his senior management to sign a contract with our company despite his personal opposition to doing so. Not to be outdone, was a customer executive from another company who chafed at heading up a project that he didn't like or believe in. (I have found that if there is an accelerant to a fiery relationship between customer and supplier it is the customer executive who begrudgingly comes to his role of interfacing with a supplier on a project or activity not of his choosing). Why senior management insisted on allowing this individual to spearhead the project activity is more of an indictment of the organization's leadership than of the man himself. In any event, this man was rude, petulant, and rarely even-handed in his dealings with our company. Worse, he aimed to sabotage the project at every turn. Other factors, too, can upset an otherwise stable relationship: supplier or customer employee turnover, especially in the leadership ranks; a change of business priorities; economic setbacks; and so forth. All of these have been known to inflict great harm in an otherwise healthy and synergistic relationship.

One year into a four-year agreement was enough to signal to one of our customers that he could ill afford the full complement of services he had originally signed up for. At the time of signing, the customer believed his costs would be much lower, and he now requested that we somehow lower our charges. This we could not do as we had to recover our costs and make a profit from providing the attendant services. The customer's position was not irrational. There was enough ambiguity in the interpretation of a particular warranty service we were providing to suggest there was some merit in the customer's position. The problem was how the company's spokesman behaved in interactions with our company. The man was insolent and abrasive. It made for a very hostile relationship. Our legal team liked our position in the dispute. Further, the contract provided for arbitration as a means to resolve any impasse. We chose to take a different route. We renegotiated the contract, eliminating the service in question while continuing to perform under other provisions of the agreement. The customer was then free to seek another supplier to provide the service that had been the scourge of our relationship.

The service ethic teaches us to have empathy for the customer, to anticipate the customer's needs, to respond with energy and alacrity. There is nothing in our philosophy, however, that compels the supplier organization to be the object of ridicule, abuse, harassment, or pressure tactics. Once it is clear to the supplier that these are not behaviors in isolation but rather behaviors that constitute a pattern of hostility, and having failed in genuine attempts at reconciliation, it is advisable to exit the relationship. As Steve Covey reminds us in his classic *The 7 Habits of Highly Effective People*, we either strike a win-win deal with our customers or "no deal."[21] Finally, I have also found it instructive to conduct a hard-hitting post mortem to learn why a relationship has gone awry—that there are two sides to a failed relationship may come as a revelation to some in the supplier organization—and how to preclude a similar reoccurrence.

## SERVICE IS NOT SURRENDER

A notable difference I have been able to observe between Japanese and American approaches to service is that in Japan many more workers in the organization—both vertically and horizontally—participate in making contact with the customer. You see that in department stores, gas stations, and hotels. At the Hotel Okura in Tokyo, for example, it is not unusual to be greeted by a valet, a porter, a greeter, and a manager at check in.

In one of the more powerful expositions I have ever read on the obstacles that impede the attainment of the service ethic, psychoanalyst James Hillman states that the ethical confusions now plaguing business, government, and the professions, although having many sources, result in part from pressures of efficiency as a value in and of itself: "As to service productivity; they (service and productivity) need to be kept distinct because they grow out of fundamentally different psychological attitudes, even archetypically different styles of existence. Our habitual ideas insist that to serve is closer to surrender; to produce, more like conquering. Production masters material; service submits to it."

Hillman further suggests that there is a psycholinguistic hang-up (my word) with the word *service* as it conjures up words such as *servitude* and *servility*—the exact opposite of industrial age words such as *power* and *strength* and therefore fraught with negative connotations.[22]

In truth, these hang-ups are mostly embedded in Western culture where personal individualism reigns supreme. In the East, Japan for example, personal individualism is subsumed by the concept of community. This is not to say that there is no concept of *individualism* in Japanese society, but that it embraces family, community, and nature. As such, Japanese culture subscribes to an egoless form of individualism that allows its members to *serve* because it is being done from the heart and for the greater good. There is no code of dos and don'ts in Japanese ethics; good or evil are situational and largely dependent on the individual's goodness of heart. Narrow financial interests, personal or corporate, gain little traction in Japanese society where sincerity, harmony, courtesy, confidence, and trust come first.

David Landes, professor of history and economics at Harvard University, concludes his towering work *The Wealth and Poverty of Nations*, a 1,000-year retrospective study of why rich nations are rich and poor nations are poor, by stating that culture makes all the difference. His admonition, however, is that in the hands of bad government a culture of values enabling progress and modernity will be to no avail. The experience of the Chinese in expatriate communities in the United States, and East Asia versus mainland China is a case in point.[23]

Today's business leadership has to embrace a culture born not of efficiency but of effectiveness of service. Ideas rooted in the industrial age—the customer can have a car painted any color so long as it's black—have to give way to an ethical construct imbued with values such as flexibility, open-mindedness, and responsiveness.

## IS THIS THE END OF *PERSONAL* SERVICE?

I am fond of sending flowers to people on different occasions. This is my way of expressing personal sentiments. Most of the time, I pick up the phone and place the order myself. On one occasion when I called the flower shop, the employee at the other end asked if she could help me. I said, "Yes, I would like to send some flowers." What do you think the next part of the dialogue was? You might say, well, the order taker asked, "What's the occasion?" or "May I offer you any help in the selection of flowers?" Wrong! The first question I was asked was, "What credit card will you be using, and what is the card number?" I asked why payment details were being requested before I had even ordered anything. What was her answer? "I am sorry, but that is the first thing that shows up on my order entry screen." In the next chapter, we'll talk about how an information infrastructure has to be compatible with the service mission, but in the absence of a system designed around service, a little *service sense* on the part of the worker is mandatory.

Self-checkout supermarket registers, hotel check-in kiosks, self-check-in airline ticket kiosks, hospital admission check-in kiosks, DVD rental kiosks, and ATMs all are meant to disintermediate the service or salesperson. The IHL Consulting Group reports that self-checkout installations at some retailers now account for 15–40 percent of the daily transaction volume. At some airlines, as many as 70 percent of domestic passengers are using self-check-in kiosks.[24] This technology—an amalgam of software, hardware, and communications—is now unstoppable and will grow exponentially in every sphere of commerce.

Retailers desperate to connect with the customer are also relying on digital media and digital signage. These are systems of networked LCDs or plasma screens controlled remotely with the ability to vary the advertising content message by store, location within the store, or time of day. A well-designed system can be used to inform, entertain, or educate the consumer at the point of purchase. The next-generation systems will employ facial-recognition technologies that will allow the system to roughly identify the demographics of the consumer standing before the screen. The system can then target a message most appropriate to that consumer. Again, the salesclerk is taken out of equation. These technologies, too, have a head full of steam. According to market researcher Info-Trends, there was an installed base of approximately 630,000 screens at the end of 2006, which is expected to grow at a compounded annual rate of 12 percent through the year 2011.[25]

Many merchants are thankful that technology has finally caught up with the surly, unhelpful salesclerk who drives customers away instead of enticing them to spend more of their money. Customers, too, are encouraged that they do not have to interact with a salesperson to get the information that they need. What does not bode well, however, is that the motivation behind these efforts to displace salespersons is not so much to improve service but to reduce cost, to enhance operating efficiency. In fact, in light of these technological initiatives, the result might be *less* service, not more. If service implies flexibility, understanding, responsiveness, and an ability to communicate, then I know for sure that this self-service world of man–machine interactions has set us back immeasurably. A kiosk can never supplant a competent, well-trained, well-equipped, and empowered frontline worker.

Other considerations remain. This trend toward *kioskization* is open season on the service ethic by a workforce that knows it is just a matter of time before it too is out of the picture. The cycle is self-feeding. Employers will continue to ignore the need to select, hire, train, and equip first-rate talent to serve their customers. Finally, it is not clear to me how an employer who never rallied her frontline staff around a service ethic is expected to do so with a floor staffed with androids. Where will the customer find safety, security, and privacy in this brave new world? And, besides, to which kiosk will the customer take his complaints of shoddy service?

# Power to the Front Line

People buy on emotion and justify with fact.

—*Bert Decker*
*You've Got to Be Believed to Be Heard*

Years ago when my eldest daughter attended graduate school at Northwestern University in Evanston, Illinois, I had to wait outside the bursar's office and watch through the picture windows while the staff finished their coffees. No amount of waving of the hands and arms could move the staff to action or to acknowledge that I was alive! Finally, after much waiting, I was allowed in so that I could pay my daughter's not-inconsiderable tuition bill. When I asked one of the staff members why they had ignored me, she said, "Sir, it wasn't time." Sadly, this kind of behavior is rampant in many organizations. It is the kind of behavior that reeks of organizational or individual incompetence. The effect on the consumer is one and the same: a frustrated customer with a new-found motivation to search for an alternative provider.

What would it have taken to have a staff person, for instance, open the door, and say, "I'm sorry sir, but our policies do not allow anyone to enter before such and such a time," or "Please come in and sit down sir, our bursar will be here in just a few minutes." How about the salesclerk, at the Home Depot, who when I asked the location in the store of a particular electrical fixture responded with nothing more than, "I just punched out," before walking away? Think how much more pleasant the experience would have been for the customer if the salesclerk had said, "I'm on my lunch hour, sir, but I'll page to have someone come over to help you right away."

Are these behaviors the failings of individual workers or of the organization's approach to service? We have no way of knowing.

In our first vignette above, for example, it is entirely possible that security policies strictly forbid entry into the bursar's office before normal working hours. In the second, the retailer's pay practices might enforce a certain amount of unpaid time off for lunch whether a salesclerk works during that time or not. In my view, however, neither of these hypothetical policies is consistent with the service ethic, as we discussed in the previous chapter, and thus neither has any place in a customer-focused organization. If these policies exist, they need to be abolished. On the other hand, the above examples could represent the failings of frontline workers who forget or choose to ignore the organization's avowed focus on service.

This chapter deals with the knowledge, learning, ability, and support required of the frontline worker if she is to be a faithful conduit of the customer-focused organization's service policies and practices. One more thing as we enter this chapter: Recall that our definition of the frontline worker includes anyone in the organization who interacts with a customer on a regular basis. Sales vice presidents, call-center attendants, mortgage loan officers, bank clerks, and table waitstaff at quick-service restaurants all are on the front line. Clearly, the details of how a supplier attracts, trains, and rewards each of these groups of frontline workers will differ. The one constant, however, is that each has the potential to drive customer satisfaction. This point of reference is necessary in order to appreciate the extent to which the organization must retool its policies and practices if it is to become an organization focused on the customer.

### FRONTLINE SKILLS THAT MAKE A DIFFERENCE

Psychologist Howard Gardner, whose pioneering work has rocked the field of educational psychology, reminds us that the conventional thinking on intelligence has been that humans could learn anything if only the subject matter were presented in the right way. That is a roundabout way of saying that success in education is a matter of how much money is thrown at it. Gardner's own theory is that there are seven different intelligences—linguistic, logical mathematical, musical, bodily kinetic, spatial, interpersonal, and intrapersonal—each with its own strengths and limitations.[1] Gardner's work squares nicely with the experience we encounter in educating and training the frontline worker: individuals learn in a variety of ways, and the diversity of the required skills is such that each poses its own set of educational challenges. Further, the onus for learning depends as much on the *individual* as it does on the educator or the educational system.

A relevant question in this context is whether the fundamental skills needed for successful customer interactions are strictly learnable. The answer is yes and no: some of the key skills are learnable, while others aren't. I believe I can teach a reasonably intelligent person to solve a quadratic equation or to read *El Cid* in Spanish (neither skill of which, thankfully, is needed for most work on the front line!). In contrast, I know a vice president of marketing who occasions the use of bomb throwing to make his arguments, who stands little or no chance of becoming more affable, gracious, even tempered, or fair. This man, in my opinion, cannot be trained to be anything other than whom or what he is. Why is that? I believe, like Gardner, there are different intelligences or, using the term more loosely, different skill sets at work, some more learnable than others. Technical skills or the technical details of performing a job are usually learnable. Most other skills are innate in the individual. In the case of the vice president of marketing, his interpersonal intelligence is probably at maximum capacity.

It is very difficult to predict whether a job applicant will be successful on the front line on the basis of one or more job interviews or by inspecting a candidate's resume florid with expressions of accomplishments. No. The candidate for a frontline job—perhaps any job in the organization—must have his skills tested and his background thoroughly checked. I might give an edge to an individual who has a shorter resume but who possesses relevant life experiences such as serving in the military with distinction, but the basic core of skills must always be present. Here is a survey of the skills I find most important—again, the depth of which must be in keeping with the job at hand—for work on the front line:

1. **Cognitive abilities**. To be effective as a frontline worker, the individual must bring to the job average or above-average cognitive—that is, mental—abilities. Cognitive abilities relevant to the frontline worker include conceptual reasoning, attention span, working memory, reading skills, and brain speed. At our company, candidates for frontline jobs who have made it to a final round of interviews are given a take-home, essay-writing assignment that is intended to tell us

the following: (1) whether they can critically process the information garnered during their interviews, (2) whether they have the ability to organize and develop a reasoned response, and (3) whether they have the ability to compose a credible response in writing. Candidates are given two or three days to return their response.

The actual assignment will vary from job to job and might vary from individual to individual based on the feedback of interviewers, but it is made clear to the candidate that there is no correct answer, and that, in the end, the company decides in its subjective judgment whether the response is appropriate to the question or questions asked. A sample essay question to a candidate for a sales position, for example, might go something like this: "Explain how you would factor in each of the elements of the company's mission statement into your marketing plan?" Surprisingly, few candidates pass this screen successfully for a variety of reasons having to do with their inability to listen and recall interview facts, think critically, and write cogently. In those cases when we have ignored the warning signals of a poor essay response in favor of a candidate's seemingly more attractive qualities, we have regretted our hiring decision.

Standardized testing can set the benchmark score for an ideal employee in a given enterprise and in a given job. This is not to say that the higher an applicant scores on such a test or on a given phase of the test the more qualified she is apt to be—in fact, the opposite may be true. A benchmark is important in order to set the minimum standard for admission into the ranks and to ensure that the individual has the capacity to grow and learn as the job evolves. A caution to the organization that chooses to test its applicants in this area, however, is that cognitive abilities are known to decline with age, and so scrupulous record keeping is required to ensure that the employer is administering and interpreting the tests fairly.

2. **Communications skills.** The frontline worker is a *communicator* pure and simple. Much of the work of the frontline worker involves having conversations and even negotiations with the customer. It stands to reason, therefore, that oral communications skills as well as writing and reading skills are at a premium on the front line. In contrast to the observation about the potential of there being a point of diminishing

returns with respect to cognitive abilities—that is, more is not necessarily better for a given job—the same cannot be said of communications skills. This is an area where high test scores should be most sought after.

Underscoring the need for the supplier to be selective in its hiring practices, however, consider that in a test of adult literacy conducted by the U.S. Department of Education in 2003, only 13 percent of those tested were found to be proficient in reading and comprehending prose.[2] Verbal communications delivered in a manner that is clear, crisp, concise, complete, and void of jargon or slang allow for exchanges with the customer that minimize misunderstandings, confusion, and ill will. And, nothing will choke off a supplier's potential for excellence in service more effectively than poor communications. Finally, frontline workers with a face to the customer must comport themselves appropriately. Retail store associates clad in football jerseys giving each other high fives or swapping stories of their sexual exploits, as I have been a witness to, have no place on the front line.

3. **Computer literacy and skill with numbers.** Next in priority of necessary skills are computer literacy and numerical dexterity. In the service and information age, these skills are very much in demand. Computer literacy as defined here means both knowledge of the use of computer applications, such as Word or Excel, as well as understanding the actual workings of computers. Unfortunately, training in computer literacy stresses the former to the near exclusion of the latter. Rote learning is a poor substitute to an understanding of computer fundamentals, especially in light of rapid technology product cycles. Does anyone remember Lotus 1–2–3? How about WordStar? A solid foundation in the basics of computing is a necessary complement to hands-on training to ensure that the frontline worker does not become obsolete with the computer application du jour.

As to math skills, the United States ranks near the bottom of the industrialized nations in math proficiency—ahead of only Portugal, Italy, Greece, Turkey, and Mexico.[3] So the pool of math talent available to the nation's employers is not overly generous. If this trend is not reversed, this fact alone will lead to the continued erosion of important jobs in our nation.

Having said all of this, it is difficult to generalize about the extent of the required proficiency of skills on the front line—beyond basic arithmetic—because a number of situational factors will influence the necessary skill level required of a particular job. For example, will the math need to be done with paper and pencil, calculator, computer? Will information systems and computer tools support the interaction with customers? Will the frontline worker have ready access to support staff of higher-level skills? A solid understanding of the specific computer and math skills of a particular frontline job is imperative in order to administer a standardized test to screen job applicants.

4. **Soft skills.** Think of the stages we as humans transit on the way to becoming adults. We begin with prenatal experiences; then move to infancy; proceed to school age, adolescence, and young adulthood; and finally—if we haven't messed up along the way—arrive at adulthood. Now think of the actors who influence those of us while in transit: parents, siblings, other family members, physicians, friends, teachers, pastors, employers, to name a few. Is it any wonder that an individual's grasp of the world—that is, the psychology of others—is so much a function of his life's journey?

   Soft skills or traits can be categorized as either personal or interpersonal and are absolutely mandatory for any frontline job. They include extroversion, politeness, a sense of humor, integrity, honesty, and patience. These traits exist on a continuum. At one end of the scale, for example, is the introverted individual, reserved and not very sociable; at the other end is the extrovert, gregarious and assertive. These trait expressions remain with us through life, though at times moving along their continuum. Personality tests are generally helpful—not infallible in and of themselves—in discerning the presence and strengths of desirable workplace traits in individuals and so should be administered to round out an intelligent program of preemployment testing.

This discussion and emphasis on preemployment testing is purposeful. It is indicative of the importance an employer places on a job at the front line that these positions are not filled with a hope and a prayer. The investment is more than worth it. The application of science to make testing part of the hiring process will result in less employee turnover, increased productivity, and a front line that will be better able to deliver a consistent message of service to the customer.

## VETTING THE FRONTLINE WORKER'S BACKGROUND

The next step in the candidate selection process is vetting a worker's background. The cost of hiring, training, and dismissing an employee who doesn't work out for some reason can range up to 100 percent of wages (200 percent of wages for employees of higher rank is not unheard of). Better to get it right the first time. A job applicant's background including his credit worthiness, criminal history, driving record, and work history all speak to a person's character, and a person's character is fundamental to performance on the job, especially one dealing with the public.

Resume inflation, work-history embellishments, and bald-faced lying about one's background are not uncommon. It is imperative, therefore, for the employer to sort out fact from fiction in a worker's history. On a federal level, the Fair Credit Reporting Act (FCRA) regulates background screening of job applicants. Employers also need to be aware of permissible practices in states and cities in which they do business so as not to run afoul of what at times are aggressive antidiscriminatory hiring prohibitions. In New York State, for instance, employers are prohibited from denying employment to an applicant previously convicted of criminal offenses in all but a few extenuating circumstances.

Once an applicant has authorized a prospective employer to search his background, the employer can turn to one of the many background screening services to corroborate the applicant's background. The FCRA, in an attempt to preclude erroneous data from harming an individual's job prospects, requires the employer to notify the job applicant of a pre-adverse-action disclosure. Upon receipt of the disclosure, the applicant can then clear his record by providing exculpatory information.

Background checks are also needed to keep the employer from negligent hiring liability claims. If an employer fails to discover that a job applicant had a history of criminal or other behavioral misdeeds and the individual commits the same or similar offense, then a claim of negligent liability can arise. A customer who is harmed by an employee can sue the employer for negligent hiring practices if it can be found that the employee had a prior history of such misdeeds. The best defense against a claim of negligent hiring is to produce and heed the results of a detailed history of the job applicant's background.

A thorough background check is a must if an employer is to have relevant information to conduct a meaningful and probing interview. Experienced corporate managers know the ins and outs of conducting job interviews—taking notice of the candidate's eye contact, grooming, posture, dress, body language, and so forth—so I'll dispense with the fundamentals here. What I would add, however, is that there is an increasingly large crop of interview-savvy candidates that will knock softball interview questions out of the park. That, plus the fact that frontline work is suffused with unpredictable, at times pressure-filled situations suggests that the interview questions—beyond the obligatory "what are your present job duties," "what do you enjoy about your job," and so forth—be as open ended as possible. This requires taking a more-conceptual and less-mechanical approach to the interview than most interviewers take. What we're trying to look for is the candidate's energy, ethics, and customer orientation. This can't be accomplished namby-pamby but requires tough interviewing skills by people who know intimately the job the new recruit will be performing and who therefore can ask direct and relevant questions.

One of our financial analysts recalls the time when he was interviewing for a position. When he was called in for a second round of interviews, he was expecting the interview to be heavily concentrated on the details of financial analysis. Instead, he found that much time was spent on a discussion of the company's mission and its customer focus—subjects that had been broached during the first interview. The interview proceeded as follows: "Tell me how compatible you are, as a person, with our company's values and mission?" "How would you deal with a customer, if you were handed the following set of circumstances?" "How would you advise a customer who approached you with this particular problem?" And, so on. It struck this otherwise very competent young analyst that here was something very important to the company, something he had little if any time to prepare for. He either had what it took, or he didn't. Service is not just a matter of dealing with facts but also of dealing with emotions. Skills such as the ability to listen, the display of spontaneity, good humor, and empathy all play a critical role in the quality of service encounters. As a result, a rigorous plumbing of the candidate's background in search of these skills is mandatory in the employee selection process.

The final step in the vetting of a job applicant entails screening for the use of drugs. Drug use has been shown to lead to increased rates of accidents, absenteeism, tardiness, and crime in the workplace, including the theft of corporate property. Alcohol and substance abusers, for example, are many times more likely to file workers compensation claims than nonabusers. Still, fewer than 8 in 10 companies administer preemployment drug screening tests. A so-called 10-panel test checks for the presence of 10 illicit and prescription drugs—marijuana, cocaine, antidepressants, and so forth—that account for roughly 95 percent of all abused drugs in our society today. These tests are very effective in spotting drug abuse because a specimen can yield positive results days or even weeks after an individual has used a drug.

False positives can and do occur, but these can readily be explained to the testing laboratory's medical officer. (We once had a young woman candidate for an accounting position who failed her drug test for marijuana. When she was told about the test results, she claimed that her mother was a cancer patient in Canada where she was smoking marijuana for treatment. "I think I was just exposed to the secondhand smoke," was the woman's response. I called the lab director and told him of the woman's claim. Secondhand marijuana smoke can leave traces of THC—the psychotropic substance found in the cannabis plant—in the urine for a day or two, but not enough, in any case, to trigger a positive result in a drug test. "Ask the woman if she has any other theories," was the director's retort!) The cost/benefits of conducting such drug-screening tests are indisputable: one unhappy incident can justify the cost of such a program for years to come.

## ALIGNING FRONTLINE PERFORMANCE TO THE SERVICE ETHIC

Leadership's role in supporting the frontline worker is indispensable if excellence in service is the expected outcome. No matter the skill and competence of the front line, without active support from executive management, it is all for naught. Here then are some of the more crucial responsibilities of executive management in aligning worker performance to the service ethic:

1. **Eliminate dead-end performance appraisal systems.** Formal, once-a-year performance appraisal systems are another legacy of the industrial-age mind-set: a system meant to

underscore the power of supervisors and managers over their subordinates. These systems have generally not been shown to enhance employee work performance over the long term, while they have proved very costly and disruptive to administer. Performance appraisal systems simply represent another feel-good bureaucratic process, and most organizations undertake them for no other reason than they've always done it that way. The underlying premise of performance appraisal systems is flawed: the employee's performance objectives must be stated in *strict* and *specific* terms such that they can be measured at the end of the year. This premise flies in the face of the broad parameters the customer-focused provider gives its front line in order to drive customer satisfaction.

What is measured and how it is used in a reward system *does* have deep implications on employee behavior. Employees should be rewarded in large part for serving the customer. Sheer hard work or individual technical virtuosity, punctuality, dependability, or a friendly attitude—the stuff of the classic performance appraisal system—should never be sufficient to propel a career forward. Individuals should enjoy the spoils only if their job performance is in keeping with the corporate mission of serving the customer. Employees uncertain about what is expected of them can be reoriented through a *performance management* system that reaffirms behaviors consistent with the mission—not once a year, but *continuously*. In our mission, *service, quality, partnership,* and *ethics* each forms the basis for measuring relevant employee performance attributes.

2. **Institute a system of rewards consistent with the mission.** Employees are committed to their world of work primarily for the rewards they derive as individuals, which in turn permits them to pursue their personal goals. There is a strong connection between the efforts of employees in achieving an employer's goals and the rewards the employees obtain for their part. The key to ensuring this connection lies in making the employer's goals congruent with the employee's rewards. Typically, this is done by linking the desired results of the supplier with the rewards employees seek for their involvement in the organization. A customer-focused supplier must operate as a meritocracy, promoting and

otherwise rewarding its most important individual contributors: employees whose work helps the supplier achieve its mission. An employee who simply does his job does not merit anything other than a standard pay and benefit package.

Rewards are either intrinsic or extrinsic. Intrinsic rewards are given by the individual to himself and reflect the employee's evaluation of his own performance. Some employees will feel rewarded because they have a chance to work with like-minded peers they appreciate and respect, or because they work for companies deemed to offer valuable products and services to the marketplace. Others will derive great satisfaction from serving customers in need. Frontline workers in health care, for instance, derive great satisfaction from doing a good job for a good purpose. Intrinsic rewards, therefore, can have a strong influence on the employees' conduct and performance, and tenure with the employer.

Extrinsic rewards come from persons other than the employee—the employee's boss, for example, or a colleague or a customer. The most common extrinsic rewards are financial in nature. It is clear that the frontline worker the customer-focused provider is attempting to attract and retain—those who meet the performance benchmarks stated earlier—is going to command wages and benefits above the norm for a given job. This is money well spent. Other financial rewards can take the form of incentives tied to the employee's efforts to enhance customer satisfaction: compensatory time off, pay increases, bonuses, or gift certificates. More generous programs can include stock option awards if these are available. Unsolicited customer testimonials—those that praise the worker for going above and beyond the call of duty—if rewarded in a generous, timely, and public fashion, can be a potent force in motivating desirable behaviors.

Extrinsic rewards can also be nonfinancial. I have used a wall of service excellence to call out the performance of an employee's truly meritorious actions. Having a plaque with your name hanging on the wall for all to see is indeed an honor. At the time a plaque is added to the wall, employees are celebrated for their work before their peers and are given a replica of the plaque. Finally, many workers consider themselves special when they participate in a company-sponsored program of continuing education. Employers should, therefore, view such a program not only as a means to enhance productivity—the putative reason behind a program of employee education—but as a legitimate perquisite to reward desirable behaviors.

Now, before anyone rushes pell-mell to develop a set of incentives, however, consider the following: if the link between service and rewards is not well designed and administered, the entire process of creating set outcomes will fail. The airline that asked their flight attendants to sport buttons asking passengers to vote for their good service—leading some flight attendants to aggressively seek votes—forgot this valuable lesson. In the end, the airline did not get its expected behaviors as passengers derided their employees' hucksterism.

3. **Exhort a customer focus as a *self-fulfilling prophecy*.** Sociologist Robert Merton coined the term to mean that people will behave as labeled for better or for worse.[4] Perceptive teachers and managers have long known the power of the so-called Pygmalion effect to motivate students and workers to achieve desired standards of performance. In *Pygmalion*, George Bernard Shaw's play, Eliza Doolittle, the poor flower girl, points out that whether she becomes a duchess has more to do with how she is treated than on what she learns. In other words, leaders must express confidence in their frontline workers to become customer-focused, to firmly set those expectations, and to demand of the frontline worker behavior that is consistent with those expectations.

4. **Empower the frontline worker to act in the customer's behalf.** Given our construct of the service ethic—to be customer driven at every opportunity—it may not be possible to give the frontline worker exact directions and goals to govern every circumstance. Empowerment in a practical sense then means that while policies serve to provide a baseline for action, their *interpretation* depends on practical considerations, situational factors, judgment, and common sense.

Here is an example: A company's policy clearly states that merchandise cannot be returned after 30 days. A customer calls and says that he has been in the hospital—or that he has been traveling to Europe on business, and so forth—for the last month, and that once he had a chance to open the package, he realized the merchandise he ordered was not what he had in mind. He would like to return the merchandise. A frontline worker with a mindless adherence to policy would say, "Sorry, our policy is no returns after 30 days." An empowered frontline worker might say, "Our policy is such and such, but we would be happy to give you credit for your purchase if the merchandise is in its original condition." Even if the customer is lying about being in the hospital, the frontline worker has made the right decision by not antagonizing a current and potentially future customer.

In the end, the customer-focused supplier is well advised to avoid micromanaging the actions of a carefully selected and trained frontline worker. Further, misguided actions by frontline workers acting of their own volition should be highlighted for process improvement and never for retribution. Empowering the employee to act in the customer's best interest has to have more than symbolic value. It must also make sense. The story of the receptionist at the Saturn automobile dealer who left her desk and drove her car to help a customer who had locked herself out of her car with the motor running has an element of human drama. Leaving a reception desk unattended, however, is not my idea of the kind of empowerment I'd like to see repeated too often!

5. **Eliminate inane policies and practices.** A bank's unwavering policy to charge customers $30 for overdraft fees risks sparking a conflagration between customer and frontline worker, potentially resulting in the loss of a customer. By the time the angry caller engages the frontline worker, she not only wants her charge refunded, but she wants to know what genius at the bank decided to charge $30 for a $5 overdraft! Now comes news that banks are charging a fee of $35 or more not only if customers don't have the funds in their accounts when the transaction clears, but merely if they don't have the funds in their accounts at the time they *sign* for their debit card purchase.[5] This practice, as well as one where banks process transactions in descending dollar order so as to trigger overdrafts more often, is inane as well as unethical. Overdraft fees are big business for banks—in 2007 banks collected $45.6 billion in overdraft fees from consumers—but bad policies are rarely forgotten by customers. How much better it would be to craft a *minimum* of policies with a *maximum* of flexibility to allow intelligent service work to take place at the front line.

Here is another one of my favorite inane policies, one I encountered personally. ADT is the largest electronic security systems and services company in the United States. If a customer has a problem with his alarm system, he calls technical support, and a technician is usually dispatched within a couple of days. The technician then is scheduled to show on the appointed day within a four to five hour window. If the customer requests of the dispatcher that the technician call first, perhaps to give the home owner who might happen to be out of the house time to meet the technician, he is met with the following rebuff: "Sorry, we can't do that." I leave for the reader to decide where best to begin the discussion of customer focus with this company.

### SUPPORTING THE FRONT LINE WITH EDUCATION AND TRAINING

Fewer strategies are as emblematic of the customer-focused supplier as those that channel investment dollars, executive time, and corporate effort toward the improvement of its human capital. It is clear that workers get a morale boost and feel better about themselves when they speak with confidence and knowledge about their company's products and services. The employer, of course, benefits by having a productive and high-performance individual represent the company. It is unfortunate, however, that frontline training programs—beyond new-hire orientation sessions—are the exception and not the rule in today's enterprise. The arguments usually made that training is expensive and time consuming fail to take into account the cost of hiring, separating, and replacing a poorly skilled worker. And, significant though these costs are, they pale in comparison to the damage an incompetent worker can cause in his interactions with customers. An intelligent program of continuing education should be designed to sharpen the worker's abilities so that, in the end, the individual is operating at a stage that in learning theory is referred to as *unconscious competence*. This final stage of learning finds a worker's skills executed largely instinctually.

The key areas to be included in a comprehensive program of continuing worker education are as follows:

1. **Skills refresher training.** No matter how proficient a frontline worker, continuous refresher training and development

in all of the skill areas mentioned earlier in this chapter will improve an individual's performance. Conferences, seminars, workshops, video blogs, and simulations can supplement conventional, potentially boring classroom training. Case-study discussions, based on actual recorded customer interactions, are also highly effective in reducing theory to practice. Certifications including the award of certificates of achievement can be issued to workers as they climb a ladder of progressively more challenging course work—from introductory to intermediate to advanced subject matter—as a way to generate excitement for their participation in continuing education.

Certifications are especially helpful in job settings that are evolving rapidly due to changing policies, practices, or technology. Finally, accomplished frontline workers should be called upon to lead training sessions based upon their subject matter expertise. This has the following benefits: (1) the presenter's skills will be further honed—there is no better way to learn a subject than to have to teach it—(2) leading a class will be seen as a special reward for good work done; and (3) presenters, taken from their own peer group, have been known to better connect with an audience in classroom settings.

2. **Product knowledge.** A frontline worker must have an intimate knowledge of the supplier's products and services or have the means to tap such expert knowledge readily. In the previous chapter, we discussed how retailers are hell-bent on rolling-out self-service kiosks and digital media to provide service and information on their products. It is no wonder. Frontline workers who don't know the product they are selling run the gamut from the esoteric—the Mercedes Benz salesman who is not able to satisfactorily explain what active body control (ABC) is (a system of sensors and microprocessors that controls the suspension's hydraulics to minimize body roll)—to the mundane, such as the chap behind the fish counter who doesn't know whether the salmon he's selling has been dyed red (i.e., if it's farm raised). A frontline worker who is not able to intelligently represent his company's products and services runs the risk of earning the consumer's ire as well as potentially forfeiting a sale for the supplier.

There was a time during the early 1990s when you could not get a martini served in a martini glass at one of the bars of that grande dame of hotels, the Waldorf Astoria in New York. The cocktail, incredibly, was served in a brown tumbler! Not a few patrons refused to drink their martinis out of a tumbler. Perhaps more damaging, however, is the lasting effects such negative impressions have on the consumer. For example, I have become conditioned to not seek help from associates working the floor in my neighborhood supermarket—part of the largest supermarket chain in the South. The young associates, including supervisory help, who work there simply don't know their store's merchandise, or if they do, they don't know where the merchandise is located. If I don't see the product I'm looking for, I don't bother to ask, I just walk.

3. **Service processes.** "How do I get credit for merchandise I returned," I asked the catalog salesclerk on the phone, "the debit for which continues to show on my statement?" This simple request began a cavalcade of, at times, spirited telephone calls, faxes, and e-mails that continued for three months before the offending debit was finally dispatched. Ask your credit card company how it computes the exchange rate on foreign transactions. If you get any satisfaction, then the gods have looked down upon you! How is this possible? The answer is that policies and practices, if they are codified, are not passed along to the front line in an intelligent manner. You cannot lock up new hires in an orientation session for two days and expect that they will graduate proficient in anything but the most basic of company processes. The most important thing the supplier can do here—again, in addition to continual training—is to provide easy access, perhaps via the company's intranet, to the entire corpus of relevant company policies and practices.

An effective continuing education program must be an ongoing effort—that's why we call it *continuing education*. It cannot be episodic or summoned only when there is a problem. On February 26, 2008, Starbucks closed its 7,100 stores nationwide for three hours to retrain all in-store employees. Chairman Howard Schultz said at the time that he was committed to "reinvent and reinvest in training the likes of which we have not done."[6] There were cynics—including many employees who charged that they were overworked and underpaid—who believed the Starbucks action was merely a public relations stunt to prop up a sagging stock price. Indeed, the share price dropped nearly 50 percent in less than a year's time prior to the shutdown. It did not occur to these skeptics, however, that perhaps the stock plunged *because* of poor service.

Finally, the responsibility for conducting education and training sessions cannot be left in its entirety to the training department or the human resources department. Earlier we noted the value of reaching into the pool of human resources on the front line to lead training sessions. The same can be said of supervisors, managers, and executives: the best training professionals in the world do not carry the street savvy of leaders who are responsible for the success of the enterprise, nor do they have the authority to effect changes in policies and practices based on what they have heard in the classroom.

## DEPLOYING COMPUTER SYSTEMS THAT INFORM THE FRONT LINE

Information accuracy, currency, and rapid retrieval are indispensable in the information tool kit of the frontline worker. Meaningful and credible exchanges with customers are not possible unless these system elements are present in the supplier's choice of operational software, whether it's third party or homegrown. Furthermore, the choice of software must rest on a dependable *common* computing infrastructure. Disparate computing platforms, perhaps the legacy of enterprise mergers and acquisitions, shortsighted system planning, sloppy system design, or lax data-architecture standards can defeat the critical system *interoperability* required to effectively support the frontline worker. Not only can this lack of harmonization of systems wreak havoc with the front line's ability to respond quickly and accurately to customer inquiries, but it can also introduce a serious loss of worker productivity.

An infrastructure designed to minimize outages caused by software errors, data incompatibilities, hardware malfunctions, environmental catastrophes, and operator mishaps will, no doubt, represent a significant investment on the part of the enterprise. A failure to act, however, can result in serious customer dissonance. Here is a case in point where you might not expect one.

I had occasion to sponsor a group of information technology executives to Offut Air Force Base near Omaha, Nebraska. The base is the location of the U.S. Strategic Command, the nation's major nuclear deterrence force on land, sea, and air. STRATCOM, as the command is called, was then run by Air Force General Lee Butler. General Butler was affable and always sported a friendly smile. The general was a real top gun. He finished first in flight school and flew F4 fighter missions in Vietnam. The general had an awesome responsibility to keep half of the civilized world from being incinerated in a thermonuclear storm. It was rumored that his advocacy on limits to the proliferation of nuclear arms contributed to his being passed over to replace General Colin Powell as chairman of the Joint Chiefs of Staff.

In any event, he was very hospitable and led the group on a tour—tours that are no longer conducted for security reasons—of the Command Center buried several stories underground and equipped with a dizzying array of technology. The general explained that part of the mission of the command included surveillance and reconnaissance to ensure U.S. vital interests were free of enemy threats. At the end of the tour, the general asked for questions, all of which were readily answered. I then raised my hand and asked a question that, although innocuous on the surface, might indicate whether our armed forces were on top of their game, "General, what is the ambient temperature over Moscow at this moment?" The general turned to a colonel and repeated the question. The colonel, in turn, asked another officer. After a few anxious moments and hushed conversations among the officer staff, the general announced: "Unfortunately, we don't have that information at the present time." Was this a case where the weather satellite used by STRATCOM was not able to communicate with the general's control center? I must admit my confidence was shaken at the general's response.

Other examples are perhaps less weighty but important nonetheless:

1. On December of 2004, Comair Airline's crew-scheduling system crashed in the middle of the Christmas holiday season as it could not handle the volume of cancellations and reschedules caused by severe weather.[7] Thousands of passengers were stranded, but despite the uproar from customers, there was little the front line could do without a working system!

2. The next time you shop at your favorite supermarket or department store and have to wait minutes between the time your groceries are scanned to the time you have checked

out—never mind the time you stood in line waiting to get checked out—be reminded that over 25 percent of the installed base of point of sale (POS) terminals is 10 years of age or older. It is no wonder these systems choke searching the correct stock-keeping unit (SKU), the latest price, the appropriate discount coupon, or simply waiting on the results of a credit card swipe.

3. In chapter 3, I discussed our company's failed attempt to build a community-wide electronic medical record (EMR) in the city of Omaha. Unfortunately, the state-of-the-art system interoperability in our nation's health care system can only be described as primitive. If you have any doubts, consider that a patient who visits a dialysis clinic, an imaging center, and his family practitioner will have left behind three completely different and scattered data sources on his medical condition. It is little wonder physicians look to the day when the exchange of medical information in electronic form will play an important role in improving the quality of patient diagnoses and treatment options.

Information that is accurate, current, and quickly accessible earns the customer's trust when it is present and available to the frontline staff. Leave any of these elements out, and the supplier runs the risk of losing customer trust and confidence. "What do you mean you can't find my payment?" fulminates the customer, "I mailed my check 10 days ago." There is no way to tell where the system broke down in this example, but it certainly did, and it proved to be a service embarrassment to the supplier.

Information systems cannot be responsive unless they rest on responsive business processes. If shipped merchandise or returns are stuck in warehouses and depots, programming elephants on the head of a pin will not make for an effective operational software system capable of supporting a high-performance frontline staff.

The principal out-of-pocket expenditure of the customer-focused provider is people. The investment in a crack front line, however, has to be matched by a commensurate investment in computer systems and tools—hardware, software, and telecommunications. The investment is not only substantial, but it must be recurring. Our company spent several million dollars approximately a decade ago developing a project management and collaboration system tailored for specific use with our customers. At the time, the system was best of breed. It was only a matter of a few short years, however, before the system became obsolete forcing us to invest in a new generation of systems. Great people with mediocre systems render the former impotent. The customer-focused provider, therefore, needs to be as determined about the deployment of effective computer systems as he is about the selection of a first-rate front line.

The frontline worker is many times the lightning rod for the lousy service we as customers receive. And, many times, that criticism is justified. Just as often, however, executive leadership is to blame as they cast the frontline worker in a no man's land devoid of systems, policies, or practices that are sure to earn the customer's ire. The responsibility for an infrastructure of support to the customer lies squarely with executive leadership. It stands to reason that the frontline worker can be no more responsive than the limitations inherent in his support systems allow him to be.

## BUSINESS TO BUSINESS: ENTER SERVICE MANAGEMENT

Much of what we have discussed in this chapter so far applies to the practice of service delivery in general. Business-to-business commerce—any commerce where one business sells to another business—requires the customer-focused supplier to take service practices to a higher level. This is the reality of having to deal in large dollar transactions with a comparatively small number of oftentimes sophisticated customers. A key organizational requirement of the customer-focused supplier engaged in business-to-business commerce is the establishment of the *service management* function. In business-to-business, service management is a function as vital as any on the organization chart. After the sale, especially, the service management organization—ever alert to shifts in customer needs and requirements—can be very influential on the direction and success of the supplier. The term *service* in service management signifies its customer focus. The term *management* implies that active participation is required of the organization in serving the customer before, during, and after the sale.

The service management function has to be organized with the following requirements in mind:

1. **Representation at the highest level possible in the organization.** The service management function has to have power. This power, in a formal sense, comes from having the organi-

zation reporting to a top leadership position in the company. Power equalization with functions of the business such as sales, finance, and operations is vital if the customer is to be given a strong voice within the supplier organization. Generally, the higher the level of a position in the organizational structure, the greater the power of that position's formal authority. In service management, this power is necessary when seeking the cooperation of various internal supplier organizations to coalesce around a given service initiative on behalf of the customer. Without strong formal authority, the service management function is ineffective. My preference has always been to have the executive responsible for service management report directly to the CEO.

2. **An independent chain of command**. Independence implies self-governing, free from the influence or control of others, and self-reliant. This independence is designed to provide a counterbalance to areas of the business that may, at times, lose their customer focus. This clearly establishes service management as the principal advocate for the customer within the supplier organization.

3. **A support organization of very well-rounded staff members.** The key to the real power that accrues to the service management organization is not so much a function of its lofty position on the organization chart. Its power—its influence—within both the customer and supplier organizations comes from trusted professionals, expert at what they do, armed with accurate information, who interpret the facts regarding service to the customer with scrupulous objectivity.

It makes no more sense for a customer-focused supplier selling to other businesses to lead an organization devoid of the service management function than it does to consider staging a production of *Hamlet* without the prince of Denmark! Yet the service management function—staffed at the executive level and with a clear service mission—is rarely found in supplier organizations.

## THE CUSTOMER ACCOUNT MANAGER

The service management function calls for a uniquely qualified group of staff professionals. These individuals must be very knowledgeable of the supplier's services, delivery mechanisms, policies, and practices; they must have a pleasant bedside manner and have higher than average communication and coordination skills. They must also have what psychologist Robert Sternberg calls *tacit knowledge*, or the ability to know what to say to whom, when to say it, and how to say it.[8] In addition, the curiosity and dogged determination of a newspaper beat reporter—obsessive about checking and cross-checking the facts—is called for by this position.

It has been my practice to give this position the title of customer account manager. Each customer is assigned a primary and, if necessary, a secondary customer account manager whose principal responsibility it is to represent the customer's interests within the supplier organization and to do so throughout the term of the relationship. The customer account manager monitors service levels and stays informed of problems or changes that need to be communicated throughout the supplier or customer organization.

At the end of the day, the principal charge of the customer account manager is to *know thy customer.* Here are some of the important responsibilities of the customer account manager:

- Participates in presales activities promoting the supplier's service practices.
- Oversees the relationship with customers with a focus on overall customer satisfaction.
- Serves as both a formal and informal point of contact with the customer.
- Maintains a detailed customer profile—the customer's leadership structure, businesses, products, finances, newsworthy developments, and so forth.
- Coordinates service initiatives.
- Monitors performance and billing under a contract or other agreement.
- Monitors service levels.
- Coordinates customer-satisfaction surveys.
- Identifies after-sale opportunities and reports the findings to the supplier's sales organization.
- Serves as a consultant to both the supplier and the customer.
- Is watchful of competitive threats that may challenge the supplier's incumbency.

The customer account manager's role is truly a role of integration between the customer and the supplier. To effect integration, this position brings together both formal power (authority) and expert power (knowledge). Inasmuch as the customer account manager has position clout, the real influence of the position internally as well with the customer comes from the ability to exercise expert power. Over time, it is crucial for a customer account manager to advance the influence of her position more by what she knows than by what she does. Ideally, the customer account manager knows more about the customer—their organization, their activities, their problems—than almost any other supplier employee, often more than many customer employees. It is a thing of beauty to see, as I have seen, when a roomful of customer executives turn to the supplier's customer account manager for a better understanding of their *own* business processes!

It is through the efforts of the customer account manager that a partnership, a community, is created between the supplier and the customer. The existence of such a partnership is not to say that customer and supplier participants will proceed to make their own decisions based on individual priorities. These priorities are almost sure to clash. It is the role of the customer account manager to act as mediator in these cases and to help chart a course that is fair to all participants.

The customer account manager position requires a lot of face time with the customer to be effective. To support a large customer account, in fact, the customer account manager must be on the customer's premises full time. This is done for several good reasons: (1) to provide the opportunity to interact with the customer formally but also spontaneously, (2) to see the supplier's service from the customer's point of view, and (3) to preempt early problems.

Where I have seen this position fail it has been because the account manager was lulled into believing that by virtue of his physical proximity or access to the customer, information, issues, and problems would somehow land on his lap effortlessly. Physical proximity or access can also lead the account manager to assume that a sense of intimacy has been established, which in the end proves false because the customer plays by a different set of rules. Decoding a customer's true intentions is a very real part of the account manager's job description.

Loyalty to the customer at the expense of loyalty to the supplier—a business version of the Stockholm syndrome—is a very real condition that I have seen develop and that requires vigilance by the executive in charge of service management. Blind advocacy on behalf of the customer is *not* the role of the customer account manager and is certain to compromise his own effectiveness as well as the supplier's.

## ACCOUNT MANAGER IN NAME ONLY

The title of account manager has been around for some time. If you ask, some companies will acknowledge the presence of staff members with this position title or some variant thereof. To clarify whether the moniker applies to the same job function that we have described as that of customer account manager, a question can be asked to serve as a litmus test: is the position's role and function *focused* on achieving customer satisfaction? If the answer is no, then the position serves some other—perhaps not unimportant— corporate function. It is not, however, that of service management.

Some companies, too, analogize the work of the customer service department with that of service management and, by extension, the work of the customer service representative with that of the customer account manager. The two, however, could not be further apart. The account manager is a customer advocate, proactively engaged to ensure maximum customer satisfaction. The customer service representative's advocacy, at times uncertain, engages only to contain customer disaffection.

Are these merely distinctions without a difference? Customer service departments are the antithesis of service management. Back-end, reactive management of customer grievances, most of which will never be brought to senior management's attention, is futile. Such complaint departments represent the weakest form of service expression and thus should be abolished.

The design of organization suggested here for the service management function will, inevitably, produce tensions with other functional departments of the supplier organization, most notably, marketing, sales, finance, and the departments responsible for the actual delivery of service. This tension, however, is by design and, in most ordinary instances, is good for the organization focused on the customer. In the end, the presence of a well-executed service management function sends a strong message to the customer that it truly has a formidable ally within the supplier organization.

## SERVICE LEVERAGE COMES FROM THE FRONT LINE

There are cases where customer expectations of performance are met or exceeded in areas of the business that have little or no impact on the customer's perception of value. This might seem contradictory, but think again. In chapter 3, we mentioned that passenger dissatisfaction with the airlines was due more often to discourteous crew members than to the quality of the aircraft, reservation procedures, or even the airfare. In these cases, the enterprise is well advised to take an in-depth look at the direct cost elements required to serve the customer. It is entirely possible, highly probable in the airline case, that service is consistently subpar because the airlines insist on making investments in areas that have little or no influence on the customer's perception of service. We cited research in chapter 3 that suggested that the rank order of service elements considered important by the enterprise was *inverted* from the customer's point of view! That situation can only come about when the supplier fails to know her customer.

If there is a strategic business reason to do so, or if the added service comes at little or no cost to the supplier, then the added service level can continue to be provided. Otherwise, these costs represent wasted capital that might best be channeled to areas or customers in need of service improvement. Before any moves are made to rationalize costs, however, a well-thought-out plan of action must be crafted, checked, and double-checked to ensure that any prospective cost saving does not lead to reductions of service below desirable benchmarks.

Finally, the frontline worker is the one resource that almost universally leaves the most lasting impression on the customer of the supplier's quality of service. Yet, as we have noted, some of the organization's weakest performers are found in these positions. Less than thorough hiring practices, meager compensation, and anemic training all are clearly inconsistent with the tenets of the customer-focused supplier as discussed in this book, but they also represent false economies. In the airline case, as in other industry examples, a competent frontline worker, *dollar for dollar*, gives the supplier the greatest lever to leave customers with a positive service experience.

### EVERYONE WORKS FOR THE CUSTOMER

I took an electronic transfer transmittal to my bank's local branch—the bank is one of the largest commercial banking institutions in the United States. I implored the private banking clerk to ensure the wire was sent before 2 P.M. as the funds were needed to cover payroll. "No problem, Mr. Pupo, all I have to do is hit *send*," said the clerk. You can guess the rest: the wire was not sent on time, and payroll was missed to the dismay of many workers. When I returned to the bank, I reminded the clerk what she had told me. "Yes, the procedure is very straightforward," said the unapologetic banking clerk. "I just got so busy; I didn't get around to sending your wire." The branch manager apologized, but all she could do was to look at the clerk and simply roll her eyes.

No supplier function has a monopoly on service to the customer. The front line, the delivery organization, and, in business-to-business commerce, service management all have their assigned roles and, it is true, do most of the heavy lifting in serving the customer. This is not to say, however, that other corporate functions are immune from the potential to provide service to the customer. A customer's perception of service quality is a complicated mosaic. It is an accumulation of moments of truth encountered by the customer, and these originate from just about any department in the supplier organization. Accounting, credit, purchasing, information technology, all have been known to leave either a positive or negative impression of service on the customer.

I have for years operated a program called Customer Connect whereby personnel in various functions, especially those with only occasional customer contact, reach out to the customer to offer any necessary assistance and to listen to opinions, feedback, and suggestions. The goal of the program is to ensure that anyone in the organization with the potential to help the customer, in any way, is given the opportunity to explore these possibilities. The program is most effective when the supplier reaches deep into the organization and causes a dialogue to happen when one, in the normal course of business, might not occur. The point is to probe, to listen carefully, and to seek out where the customer has a problem—whether or not it is supplier-related or caused, for the supplier might have an answer to a problem that has eluded others. These interactions begin slowly—almost coolly they are so unexpected—but over time, they can develop into important two-way channels of communication as they reaffirm the supplier's empathy and genuine desire to help. The Customer Connect program, or some variant thereof, can be an important weapon in the arsenal of service to the customer, giving full force and effect to the supplier's objective that service is *everybody's* business.

# V

# Musings on the Economics of Service

> People can decide whether to pick apples or plant apple trees.
> In the first case there are more apples today; in the second,
> more apples tomorrow.
>
> —*Steven Landsburg*
> *Price Theory and Applications*

In the first half of the 19th century, Jewish immigrants from Germany noticed that in the then hinterlands of Pennsylvania, citizens could not conveniently shop for their preferred items. The only way they had to obtain the goods they needed was by making long and arduous wagon rides to distant towns to shop.[1] The bearded and scruffy peddlers, ever vigilant to the needs of the community, intuitively realized what many of today's MBA-adorned marketing executives don't—namely, that *service sells*. The peddlers noticed the goods that moved and simply brought them to the doorstep of the consumers living in the outlying areas. If an item was needed in a particular area, the peddlers were willing to walk to the nearest town where the merchandise was available, buy it, and bring it to where it was needed. The convenience was too good to pass up, and it called for a premium price.

Later, these indefatigable peddlers broadened their selling strategy by extending credit to customers they got to know. Over time the territories in Pennsylvania became saturated with competing peddlers, so many took their businesses elsewhere. The more enterprising peddlers, once again, broadened their strategy and in order to extend their marketing reach bought horse and wagon and, in essence, put their store on wheels.[2]

The shopping conveniences provided by the intrepid 19th-century peddler created sufficient differentiation from other shopping experiences available to the consumer of the time that it precluded the only reasonable substitute—the wagon ride to the center of town.

## SERVICE AS A DIFFERENTIATING STRATEGY

The service differentiation created by the early peddlers, though it came at a higher price, was sufficient to dampen the elasticity normally associated with the price/demand of commodity products or services. Conventional price elasticity of demand sees volume fall off as consumers seek substitutes or go without in the face of price increases. The door-to-door salesmen—we'll drop the peddler moniker with its negative connotation—in our example not only developed an innovative shopping service, but they also developed a way to defend their higher prices. Generally, the less differentiated—or, in other words, the more commoditized—the product or service, the easier it is for the consumer to comparison shop with the consequent risk to the supplier of a lost sale to a substitute provider. On the flip side, greater differentiation means less head-to-head comparisons are possible and thus a lessened risk of loss.

Buyers must perceive significant differences in aesthetics, features, functions, quality, or any of a score of other attributes so as to place greater value on the differentiated product. For products of roughly equal features and functionality, service quality can be the tipping point that wins the consumer's business. Bank checking accounts, for instance, have become highly commoditized. Is there any way to differentiate a checking account? Most checking accounts in the United States are free so that price as a particular differentiator is used up. What if the bank offered discounted travel insurance to checking account customers who kept a minimum balance in their accounts? What if the bank offered discounts for concerts, sporting events, and restaurants? What if the bank forgave overdrafts? (I know, I'm getting carried away.)

What attributes, in fact, constitute a tipping point? As we noted in chapter 2, product and service design initiatives must be rooted to the customer experience. That is, no intelligent product or service differentiation strategy is viable unless, in the end, it is the outcome of listening to the customer's voice.

## CUSTOMER SATISFACTION AND PROFITABILITY

Exactly how a supplier's customer-satisfaction ratings impact the profitability of the business has preoccupied management researchers and scholars who, for decades, have sought to establish this connection in mathematical terms—that is as a correlation of one variable, satisfaction, to the other variable, profit. Some researchers have found that changes in customer-satisfaction ratings generally move in the same direction as changes in a company's stock price.[3]

That a correlation can be found regardless of a company's capitalization, industry, or competitive market is not highly likely as myriad phenomena get in the way of establishing the connection in no uncertain terms. Even if a strong correlation were found, moreover, it is not clear that we would be out of the woods in explaining how customer satisfaction *causes* higher profits.

A customer's judgment of a supplier's overall service depends on his transactional experience—that is true. But it also depends on his experience with the supplier's organization in areas unrelated to the delivery of service—the supplier's accounting or credit organization, the supplier's standing in the community, and so forth—the price paid for the goods or services, the customer's own behavioral preferences, competitive options, and a number of other situational factors. Business profitability is similarly complex as it depends on issues that go far beyond service delivery to include the supplier's management competence, the general financial condition of the enterprise, the state of the economy, regulatory considerations, and so on. Furthermore, how a service transaction completed in a prior period affects profitability in a current period is anybody's guess.

In my view, the search for a correlation between customer satisfaction and the profitability of the business is the equivalent of the physicist's search for a generalized solution to the three-body problem in classical mechanics—that is, predicting the position of three bodies in space all interacting with one another. That problem can only be solved by assigning arbitrary values to all of the variables that get in the way of the solution! Establishing a correlation between customer satisfaction and business profitability would clearly give those executive leaders who are still on the fence about where best to employ capital the rationalization needed to justify expenditures for service initiatives. Finding that correlation, again, is not going to happen except in cases so contrived as to be almost meaningless. What is an executive leader to do?

Why not intuit the correlation? That is, why not *assume* that service improvements that enhance customer satisfaction do lead to improved profitability? Implicit in this assumption, of course, is the organization's having full knowledge and awareness of the investment required to effect the desired service improvements. If we are wrong in our assumption—that is, if service is improved but profitability does not show an uptick—we have, at a minimum, ratcheted-up service for customers who might as a consequence become repeat buyers and who might recommend us to their friends; for the competition who themselves might have to spend more to meet our service quality standards; and, perhaps most importantly, for our own organization, which might now have to perform at a still higher level. This last consideration is a powerful dynamic I call the *service irony*. That is, improved levels of service beget higher levels of service expectations on the part of customers, which, in turn, drive the need to perform at still higher levels of service.

Needless to say, if we are right about the correlation between customer satisfaction and profitability, then we are the beneficiaries of improved financial returns to the business. Right or wrong, this is a win-win proposition, and it requires no further research.

## SERVICE QUALITY, VALUE, AND PRICE

It is standard microeconomic theory that customers seek to maximize the utility—that is, the want-satisfaction—of a product or service and the disutility of price. Further, though the measure of value is subjective from individual to individual, the value of a product or service still hinges on both its usefulness as well as its scarcity. A caution to commodity suppliers is that the closer supply comes to soaking up available demand in an industry, the more the value proposition shrinks and the more that price becomes the deciding factor for buyers.

Generally speaking, customers perceive value as a function of the benefit derived from the supplier's service in relation to the price paid for the service. This means, in principle, that a supplier can enhance value by employing one of three strategies:

1. **Leveraging service (improving or expanding service)**
2. **Lowering price**
3. **Leveraging service and lowering price**

An effective means for a customer-focused supplier to become distanced from the pack of commodity suppliers is by relying first and foremost on the lever of service to enhance value. This is not, altogether, a strategy without risk. Some buyers are responsive only to price points and thus will fail to see—or choose to ignore—how improved service enhances the supplier's value proposition to them. In the absence of price discounting, the customer-focused supplier can see the business go to a competitor who is willing to make concessions on price or who, in fact, operates a lower cost structure.

A customer-focused supplier under price pressure by a competitive supplier who has mainly the lever of price with which to impact the customer's perception of value is well advised to defend margins and force the competitor to compete on service. If that isn't possible, the customer-focused supplier can, of course, respond with its own price lowering actions, but that judgment is best made when all of the factors of the competitive situation (the marketing or strategic value of winning a customer's business, the anticipated customer life-cycle revenues, etc.) are well understood. As a rule, however, the customer-focused supplier is best served by shifting the competitive focus away from price and toward service.

Most suppliers discount price reflexibly when they find themselves in a competitive situation. Many times, suppliers are creative in disguising discounts as promotions, giveaways, and so on, but it amounts to the same thing: lowering the price to achieve a sale.

The supplier who has only the price card to play had better be *the* low-cost producer relative to its competition. This is because continuous discounting by a supplier who is not the low cost producer—but who acts like one because it hasn't figured out how to lever service to enhance its value proposition—is unsustainable and can ultimately prove ruinous. The customer, for its part, who is dependent on a no-frills, low-cost provider, may find any cost advantage nullified if the supplier's quality and service are not, at minimum, on a par with the higher-priced competitors.

## *QUO VADIS* CUSTOMER SATISFACTION?

There is no better proxy for the long-term economic potential of a business in the service and information age than the strength of its customer-satisfaction ratings. The next two sections of this chapter will explore in detail the context in which customer-satisfaction ratings are meaningful to the supplier. It is important, however, to be reminded that satisfaction ratings cannot simply be taken at face value. Here are some words of caution:

1. **Survey anomalies can present themselves in the best-conducted satisfaction surveys in ways that can limit the**

**value of the survey data.** Aggressive promotions, overzealous service representatives (incented by the provider to achieve high scores), and product discounts all have been known to spike satisfaction scores. Intelligent survey design and administration requires that the data be normalized for these presumably temporary phenomena so as to get a truer picture of customer satisfaction. In any event, the focus of management's attention with respect to raw survey data needs to be on long-term trends and patterns.

2. **A satisfied customer may not be a profitable customer.** Good survey design and administration gets behind the survey numbers in order to find a relationship between customer satisfaction and customer profitability. There may be a very good reason why a customer who does not throw off the expected profit margin is kept in the fold, but management must make such a decision fully aware of its consequences. (In a later section of this chapter, we will discuss why it might be short-sighted to cut loose the seemingly low-profit-margin customer.)

3. **Satisfied customers may or may not be loyal in the sense that they are repeat buyers**. They may speak highly of our products and services to others, and they may confirm their high level of satisfaction when surveyed, but for a variety of reasons, they may not continue to trade with us. I've had customers give us the highest satisfaction marks possible only to see them move to a competitive supplier at contract expiration. Again, good survey design and administration attempts to get behind the elixir of superior customer-satisfaction ratings looking for the repeat buyer.

So, how *do* we know where customer satisfaction is headed? Frustratingly, we never know exactly. What we do know is that customer satisfaction is principally the result of excellence in service and thus is a key differentiator for the enterprise in the service and information age.

Business initiatives designed to foster enhanced customer satisfaction need to move to the top of the list of corporate priorities. As we have discussed, moreover, so much of the conventional wisdom is to focus on short-term financial results that strong and effective leadership is necessary if service improvement initiatives are to make the priority list at all.

Customer satisfaction is a global and generally abstract measure of service. That is, it subsumes every possible customer perception of service with the supplier and as such it is context and time dependent. The upshot is that the supplier must make a serious commitment of time, people, and capital to ensure its continuous monitoring in order to provide the necessary feedback and direction to continued service initiatives. To understand and manage customer satisfaction, the enterprise needs to grasp the vagaries of how expectations are formed and how performance is viewed.

To expect is to look forward to the likely occurrence of something. Life is built around expectations. In this regard, human behavior rests largely on two major milestones: first, an expectation of something and then a comparison of the expectation with actual performance. The two dimensions—expectations and performance—set limits that are related in dynamic ways.

Customers reach judgments on their level of satisfaction by comparing supplier performance with expectations. A customer's expectations are many times set long before a customer has experienced the supplier's performance. Marketing, advertising, and promotional material as well as sales presentations and testimonials paint for the customer the initial images of the supplier's expected performance. Lofty expectations driven by savvy brand management initiatives may *attract* customers, but it is service that *retains* them.

It is the gap between expectations and perceptions that renders a customer's judgment of satisfaction. To be sure, the same service can be judged differently by different customers. More problematic, however, is that the same service can also be judged differently by the same customer as both expectations *and* perceptions change with time.

Getting a handle on the dynamic that is customer satisfaction is a key component in the supplier's attempt to understand what makes the market tick for his products and services.

## SURVEY, SURVEY, SURVEY

Physicians tell us that most people with hypertension have no symptoms whatsoever. There are no specific warning signals. The only way to find out if a person has hypertension is through regular monitoring of blood pressure. A person who takes medication or natural supplements to fight hypertension but who fails to monitor his blood pressure on a daily basis can run a huge, perhaps fatal, health risk. In our context, rolling out all of the service improvement initiatives in the world without the regular monitoring of the effect of those initiatives can run the risk of missed opportunities, customer attrition, and lost business. In the end this, too, can prove fatal.

I have worked with customer-satisfaction surveys since the 1970s, a time that clearly belongs to the prehistory of such surveys (J. D. Power and Associates, for example, conducted its first consumer satisfaction survey in 1981), and have never failed to learn from them. As a result, I place great stock and emphasis on knowing where the organization's customer satisfaction is trending. For that reason, I spend a lot of time poking and probing what our customers have to say about our service. Here are some of the different approaches I have used to take the pulse of the customer's level of satisfaction:

1. **Episodically.** Executives from the supplier organization meet face-to-face with customers at fairs, gatherings, soirees, ribbon-cutting ceremonies, customer user groups, baseball games, and so on for no better reason than to hear first-hand what the customer thinks of the service. This survey approach is asymmetric because the customer does not expect to be asked his opinion of service given the social context of the occasion. In these situations, though the feedback is anecdotal, it is also unfiltered and thus of great value.

2. **Formally.** Surveys must be administered continuously. It doesn't make sense to wait months, much less a whole year, for survey results if enterprise practices might have changed in the interim. Throughout the year, statistically significant segments of the customer set must be administered a survey containing a variety of probing questions about the quality of the service they are receiving.

3. **Event driven**. Customer satisfaction must be monitored shortly after the delivery of service—the installation of a system, the closing of a loan, and so forth. Also, significant changes in policies and procedures, such as in the areas of billing or hours of operation, provide an opportunity to gauge the customer's reaction and satisfaction with the change event—while their memories are fresh—as well as with the overall level of service.

Each survey modality or form of distributing the survey—telephone, mail-in questionnaire, face to face, or e-mail—has its strengths and weaknesses, its risks and its rewards. Each should be administered within its proper context, and no single modality should be relied upon exclusively to preclude the potential for bias. Further, customer-satisfaction surveys have to be individually and carefully tailored not only to the specific business, but very specifically to the products and services in question. Consistent survey questions and scaling are crucial if survey data are to be tracked over time. In the end, crafting a sound satisfaction survey can be tricky business and so should be left to the professionals.

Here are some of the key principles to follow in effective customer-satisfaction survey design and administration:

1. **Use a survey method in keeping with the size of the customer population.** Balancing the precision of survey results with a level of confidence in those results underscores the need not only for solid survey design but for the proper statistical handling of the survey population. In business-to-business organizations, with numerically small customer populations, it may be possible to administer a survey to the entire customer base. (What response rate the supplier might experience is another matter. Our company has been able to approximate a 90 percent response on many of its surveys by using a third-party survey firm and plenty of prodding to return responses!) In the business-to-business world, a single customer's loss can be potentially devastating to a supplier. For that reason alone, every attempt should be made to know *each* customer's level of satisfaction with all aspects of the supplier's performance. Financial and time considerations, clearly, preclude this census survey approach to organizations with large customer populations. On the other hand, a properly administered statistical sample can reasonably gauge an entire population's level of satisfaction.

2. **Use a five-point rating scale to index customer responses.** The most common of these is a Likert scale, named after psychologist Rensis Likert who developed the five-point scale in the 1930s. The Likert scale measures the strength of a negative or positive response to a statement along a continuum. At the low end, a customer who was "Very Dissatisfied" with our service would indicate a response with a numeric

value of 1. A customer who was "Dissatisfied" would indicate a response having a numeric value of 2. A customer who was "Neither Satisfied nor Dissatisfied" would indicate a response having a numeric value of 3. At the opposite end of the scale, a customer who was "Satisfied" with our service would indicate a response with a numeric value of 4. Finally, a customer who was "Very Satisfied" with our service would indicate a response having a numeric value of 5. Scales of more than five points have been shown to offer little incremental advantage to the five-point Likert scale.

3. **Seek a global rating of satisfaction.** Regardless the choice of specific survey questions such as those that might get at the customer's reaction to price, quality, and the courteousness of frontline staff, I have always insisted on asking the customer, first of all, to grade her level of overall satisfaction. This sequencing of survey questions generally keeps the overall satisfaction score from being biased by the respondent's reaction to a subsequent question dealing with a specific aspect of the service. Occasionally, a customer will give high marks on service delivery and low marks on satisfaction. (I have also found the reverse condition, but that is most unusual). What is going on here? The explanation is found in the customer's perception of service in its most global context: price, competitive options, interactions with frontline personnel, and even environmental conditions can alter a customer's opinion of the supplier when the service, on the face of it, seems consistent in its quality. The Bank of America's program of extending credit to illegal aliens caused a firestorm of opposition, which led to a call for a boycott of the bank and led many of the bank's customers to move their accounts to competitive institutions.[4]

4. **Anchor the service being surveyed**. Ask the customer to confirm that he indeed received the service in question before proceeding with the rest of the survey. We should expect a "Strongly Agree" response to the survey question, "I closed an automobile loan with the ABC Company in December 2008." This anchor question must always make explicit the service in question so there is no ambiguity as to the authenticity of the respondent when interpreting survey results.

5. **Develop appropriate and specific survey questions.** In chapter 2, we discussed the importance of proper wording in the

design of surveys meant to elicit customer feedback that might prove useful in product or service design initiatives. Survey questions designed for the purpose of measuring customer satisfaction call for the same care and attention in wording. Customer responses cannot be interpreted correctly unless survey questions or statements are specific and unambiguous. Asking a customer, for example, to "Rate your satisfaction with your recent loan transaction" can leave the survey team in the dark as multiple interpretations are possible for the words *recent* and *transaction.* Key questions that should always be included in a survey are those that ask the respondent about the likelihood that he will recommend the supplier to others and whether the respondent plans on a repeat purchase of the supplier's products and services.

6. **Ask open-ended questions as a means of sourcing ideas for service improvement**. Open-ended questions are a must in any intelligent survey instrument. Responses to open-ended questions will at times yield suggestions for legitimate service improvement or corroborate for the supplier what it is doing right. Suggestions for improvement, after an initial screening to ensure their reasonableness, need to be thoroughly investigated for their merit and the suggestions implemented as appropriate.

7. **Make taking the survey a pleasant experience.** A customer-satisfaction survey should be a reasonably pleasant experience—insofar as taking a survey can be a pleasant experience—for the participant. Telephone surveys, especially, need to be succinct and administered pleasantly, courteously, and quickly. They should also get to the crux of the matter, which is to plumb the customer's perception of service delivery, and not meander in other directions. Asking the same question in different ways in order to reinforce other survey responses runs the risk of the respondent terminating the survey prematurely. Survey takers need to be trained for the survey project at hand and be given sufficient flexibility to deal with customer feedback which may not fit neatly into the survey form.

Tiffany & Co., which renders excellent service before and after the sale, hires the Gallup Organization to conduct customer-satisfaction surveys via telephone. My experience has been that the excellent service that Tiffany provides, however, is marred by a survey that is more marketing research than satisfaction survey and is too long and stiff. A stilted survey such as I have had to endure with Gallup on behalf of Tiffany risks a *drop-off* by the respondent, which can bias overall survey results and leave the supplier without potentially valuable feedback.

What we do with the data once the survey is completed is what is most important. Here are some of the key post-survey activities that should be undertaken to make the survey data meaningful for managing the business:

1. **Careful tabulation of responses is mandatory if the supplier is to glean trends and insights that might otherwise remain hidden.** As we said earlier, high customer-satisfaction ratings might be the result of discounts or promotions that have little to do with service delivery. Having high satisfaction ratings, therefore, without knowing *why* is tantamount to playing a game of Russian roulette with the service factors that impinge on customer satisfaction. A special emphasis needs to be placed on closely examining very high or very low satisfaction scores—assuming that analysis of the results reveals that no selection biases have crept into the survey methodology—that can lead to immediate and high-impact opportunities for improvement.

2. **Cross-tabulation of survey data can take many forms, but two distinct looks at the data can be particularly helpful.** One involves contrasting and comparing the results of respondents who are very satisfied to those who are very dissatisfied on a particular aspect of the supplier's service— quality, convenience, price, and so forth. Ordinarily, the service component with the widest ratings gap offers the greatest opportunity for improvement of overall satisfaction. Thus, if convenience and quality account for a 30 percent and 20 percent difference, respectively, as rated by respondents who are very satisfied versus those who are very dissatisfied, there is a good chance that overall satisfaction will be most impacted by improvements in convenience. Also, correlating an individual survey statement rating to a rating on overall satisfaction is an excellent way to pinpoint what the customer finds most important in his dealings with the

company. If price and convenience rate low to moderately low marks, whereas quality rates high, then it is reasonable to assume that a high customer-satisfaction rating is due to quality and not the other factors.

3. **Customer-satisfaction ratings must be correlated to customer profitability.** Experience is all over the map in this area, and so it is foolhardy to come up with a bulleted list of dos and don'ts. For example, are satisfied customers less profitable that dissatisfied customers? If so, by how much? And, is the difference statistically significant? Where do the most profitable customers rank in terms of customer satisfaction? A satisfied and very profitable customer might be as much a potential defector—if the high margin is the result of a high price, the door is as good as open to a competitor—as a customer who is fed up with the supplier! And so on. Suffice it to say that customer-satisfaction ratings data must be compared to individual customer profitability in an attempt to infer important trends and patterns as a precursor to management action.

4. **Study the nonrespondent (or otherwise unsurveyed) population to ensure there is no discernible pattern that can bias the survey results.** In the absence of this kind of hard information, survey results will fail to yield actionable items required to remediate service issues. Here are two examples of what I mean:

   1. A Wachovia Bank press release published in February 2008 announced that the bank had been ranked number one, for the seventh straight year, by the American Customer Satisfaction Index (ACSI). The ACSI is a serious survey, widely quoted by the media, conducted by the University of Michigan's Ross School of Business. There is always more than meets the eye to the results of any customer-satisfaction survey, but this one is especially troubling. Consumers, again, need to take the time to separate fact from fiction of supplier claims. In chapter 1, you will recall, we discussed the egregious disregard for legal—never mind ethical—conduct on behalf of Wachovia Bank executives toward their customers. How, then, does the bank's misbehavior reconcile with the ACSI survey rankings? Let's take a look.

First, ACSI surveys only 5 banks. (I suppose being ranked number one is reason to crow, but I don't know how jubilant I would be, knowing I'm competing with approximately 7,000 other banks in the United States, including 50 with $5 billion or more in assets that were not surveyed!) Second, Wachovia's ranking of 79 points out of 100 is 7 points ahead of Bank America, a bank with $279 billion, or 67 percent, more in customer deposits. Third, the survey results, published in February 2008, hark back to survey data collected during the fourth quarter of the previous year, or about the time that many of Wachovia's deceptions were gaining public currency. Finally, the bank's mortgage, investment, and brokerage customers—the source of many of the bank's major transgressions, aside from money laundering and the unsigned check fraud—were *not* included in the ACSI survey. (If for no other reason than this, the ACSI needs to reconsider its survey methodology very seriously.) So much then for a number-one ranking!

2. IBM used to send me a questionnaire that asked how much hardware, software, and services I had bought from them since the last survey period (I have my doubts, but if IBM really didn't know how much I spent with them, that speaks to a different problem!); whether deliveries were timely; how frequently my sales representative paid a visit, and so forth. Twice in consecutive years, I wrote long and thoughtful letters—thereafter I threw the survey away—telling them what I thought of their survey; namely, that the questions posed were shallow and perfunctory and never got around to asking me what I really thought of their service. It was as if the survey takers were afraid to ask a question they might not like the answer to! Given that our company was a customer of some consequence, what would it have taken for an IBM executive to have called me on the phone and ask me what I really thought? That call never came.

Clearly, customer-satisfaction surveys are necessary in helping the supplier tune her products and services to the demands of the market. But customer-satisfaction surveys have other important uses. I have published customer-satisfaction survey results—aggregating much of the data to protect both customer as well as company confidentiality—for years as an important tool for customers to gauge their own responses vis-à-vis overall survey results. I have also used survey results as a marketing tool with new prospects not only to showcase the quality of our service as customers see it but to demonstrate an important manifestation of our customer-focused philosophy, which is that we have a keen interest in keeping the pulse of the customer base.

## CUSTOMER SATISFACTION VERSUS CUSTOMER LOYALTY

As we have already noted, a satisfied customer is not the same thing as a loyal customer. A customer is satisfied so long as the value derived from the supplier's service, in its most global sense, exceeds the price the customer pays for the service. It follows that the greater the customer's perception of value, the greater the level of satisfaction. And, if you've been with me thus far, you know that the assertion stated throughout this book is that, as a rule, a satisfied customer will reward a supplier with a long-term relationship. A satisfied customer, therefore, is the end-result of a business strategy whose focus is excellence in service.

Customer loyalty has a different genesis. A customer is loyal—is unswerving in its allegiance—if it consistently does business with a supplier. This definition holds irrespective of whether the customer has an opportunity to defect to a competitor. A customer can be loyal, therefore, given an absence of viable competitive options regardless of the reason. The lack of alternatives might be the result of unaffordable choices, customer management fiat that restricts certain supplier choices, regulatory prohibitions, or monopolistic markets.

Our company was once asked to propose a design for a data network to serve the largest private company in Venezuela. At the time, all phone service in Venezuela was nationalized—as it remains today and of uniformly poor quality. Still, our customer prospect felt that the government might actually welcome having private enterprise take on the task and expense of building its own network. The customer was delighted with our design. The next step was to present it to the authorities for their blessing. The plan never got off the blocks. A government representative explained that the state's telecommunications monopoly extended to private data networks, and that it would take a special *dispensation*—special *palm grease* might have been a term more apt—by the congress and the president to waive the rule.

(This trip was memorable from a customer service standpoint in another way. While staying at the Tamanaco Intercontinental Hotel, located in one of Caracas' most exclusive shopping and leisure districts, I became very ill with a high fever that kept me in bed for over 24 hours. I was so weak that I could not muster enough strength to reach the phone on the nightstand to call for a doctor. I thought I was actually going to die. When I recovered and stopped at the restaurant for my first meal since becoming ill, I found the source of my problem. I asked the liveried waiter for bottled water. The waiter returned with the bottle of water on a silver tray. The bottle cap had been removed and was resting on the tray next to the bottle. It suddenly occurred to me that each and every time I had asked for bottled water at the restaurant, it had been served in exactly the same way: bottle cap removed. This time, I said to the waiter, "Please bring me another bottle of water, but don't remove the cap." The waiter disappeared into the kitchen for a few minutes and when he returned he said, "Perdon señor, but the restaurant has just run out of bottled water." Ever since, I've taken many an international trip with my own bottles of water.)

Clearly, loyal customers might or might not be satisfied customers. If they are not, then an opportunity clearly avails itself for the supplier to change the perception for its products and services. Many Microsoft customers, for instance, devoid of desktop operating system alternatives (Microsoft operating systems control 3 out of every 4 personal computers of all makes, and 9 out of every 10 Intel-based machines) continue to reward the company with repeat business. This while, at the same time, expressing a great deal of dissatisfaction with many of the software giant's business practices.

Software company CA Inc. (formerly Computer Associates International) under the reign of its founder Charles Wang and his protégé Sanjay Kumar, who pled guilty to obstruction of justice and securities fraud in 2006, had a nasty reputation for browbeating customers—although, in fairness, it must be said they browbeat everyone they came in contact with, including their own employees. CA sales executives would not negotiate the terms of a licensing agreement, the price, their service responsibilities, or anything else for that matter. They would simply march into our office, drop off a contract, and state their price. It was pretty much take it or leave it. Unfortunately, CA had a lock on certain classes of software that neither our company nor others who utilized their products could do much about. Can it be said that customers in these situations are loyal? Emphatically, painfully, as a vassal is to his lord.

A dissatisfied customer, with no meaningful buyer options, can become a nightmare for the supplier. Not only is such a customer ready to bolt the moment the competitive landscape shifts, but in the interim, it is apt to engage in actions hostile to the supplier, such as participating in efforts—overtly or covertly—to disparage the supplier, resorting to litigation, and generally becoming a costly maintenance headache, all in an attempt to compensate for a position of weakness. In such a circumstance, the supplier should hope that a competitor will materialize and take the rancorous customer away!

In sum, it is a satisfied customer whose loyalty we seek. As Frederick F. Reichheld—who has done more work on customer loyalty than anyone I know—says of those who work at or buy from a particular company, "I will invest my loyalty in businesses that can deliver superior value. When value is insufficient, and when a reasonable effort to fix the problem fails to produce results, I will defect to a business where my loyalty can create better value."[5]

### J. D. POWER, WHERE HAVE YOU BEEN?

As the economy continues its headlong race toward services, customers more and more are left to their own devices in evaluating a supplier's relevant service experience. In this environment, besides the cottage industry of consumer activists and bloggers, customers will come to appreciate the assistance of third-party firms to help them separate hype from reality. Firms such as *Consumer Reports*, Angie's List, and others serve a valuable purpose in providing unbiased independent ratings and reviews.

Few suppliers, however, hire third-party firms to conduct customer-satisfaction surveys. Fewer suppliers still disclose customer-satisfaction data publicly. I have called on survey firms till I was hoarse to render such a service in the business-to-business information technology industry where supplier rhetoric and customer naiveté seem to feed off each other.

Beginning just before the Y2K software remediation rage, I was concerned that as a small company we weren't getting the attention in the marketplace that our fine work merited. We had recently launched a software development and maintenance center in Limerick, Ireland, where we sourced smart lads and lassies from just across the green at the University of Limerick, a terrific school with both undergraduate and postgraduate programs in informatics and whose dean would ask employers what subjects they thought the university should be teaching!

President John F. Kennedy's sister, Jean Kennedy Smith, U.S. ambassador to Ireland, was so excited that she helped promote and launch the venture. Our service rocked, and I wanted the whole world to know. I called just about every major research house that was out there to track customer-satisfaction ratings, but my idea just couldn't garner the interest of the researchers or the competition. The researchers were more comfortable *tiering* technology companies on the strength of their balance sheets (a Tier 1 company having a stronger balance sheet than a Tier 2 company, etc.) than on the strength of their customer-satisfaction ratings. Suppliers, of course, were in no hurry to expose a potentially weak flank of their business. I would say, "Look, if J. D. Power and Associates can call me and ask if I'm satisfied with my Cadillac, they can call and ask if I'm satisfied with my ISP service or my software maintenance provider or my payroll service company. Statistically significant data can then be aggregated, and the results published periodically." Clearly, suppliers in the space would have to voluntarily furnish customer lists from which the researchers could draw their sample. Alas, that was not to be. Since that time, J. D. Power and Associates has made much progress and become well known for their customer-satisfaction studies in business-to-consumer Internet and telecommunications services as well as in a number of other important consumer product and service areas. When it comes to business-to-business services, however, the buyer is left pretty much to his own devices.

In Japan, banks have had to be gently coerced to participate in customer-satisfaction surveys. Japanese banks, never a bellwether of excellence in service to retail consumers—banks in Japan have long relied on cozy relationships with politically connected companies for the bulk of their business—have been called to task by their oversight agency. The Financial Services Agency, which oversees the banking, securities, and insurance industries, has asked banks to include the results of customer-satisfaction surveys as part of its banking reform program. Some banks, naturally, accuse the agency of overreaching, while many, especially the larger banks, have begun to comply. Few institutions have published their findings, but there is support growing to have banks include their customer-satisfaction survey results along with their periodic financial disclosure documents.[6]

## CONSIDERATIONS IN CUSTOMER
## ACQUISITION AND RETENTION

In many companies, most brand marketing and sales expenses can be said to be costs incurred in the acquisition of new customers. It follows that if a company spends $1,000,000 in marketing and sales budget dollars to acquire 100 customers, then the cost of acquisition is, on average, $10,000 per customer. So long as this ratio holds, the marketing executive can budget additional dollars to garner a predictable percentage of additional customers. It also follows that if the company loses 100 customers over the same time period, then the marketing and sales budget is simply covering the churn. The reflex reaction by the vast majority of companies is simply to spend more to gain more customers. Customer retention, it is fair to say, always plays second fiddle to customer acquisition. That approach, though misguided, is contemporary marketing orthodoxy.

Customer attrition rates vary widely by industry—20–30 percent in telecommunications services, 10–15 percent in banking, and single digit percentages in many business-to-business sectors. The arithmetic is elementary: if a company has 1,000 customers and loses 100 of them over a given period of time, say a year, then the attrition rate is calculated at 10 percent per year. In my experience, though the math might be straightforward, few marketing executives know their own company's customer attrition rate to any degree of accuracy. This is unfortunate as it cripples the marketing executive's ability to have a sound grasp of the economics of acquiring and keeping customers. Knowing your own company's customer attrition rate is a necessary first step in gaining that understanding. Incidentally, ask the same marketing executives about their new sales opportunities, and they will wax poetic on the minutest details of their sales pipeline.

If marketing executives are generally in the dark as to their company's customer attrition rates, the consequent financial impact of such attrition remains more enigmatic. Arriving at the *average* cost of attrition per customer is simple enough. This cost can be calculated by dividing the gross profits of the enterprise (revenues minus direct costs) by the total number of customers to yield average profitability by customer. This number is then multiplied by the number of customers lost in a time period to get at the total cost of attrition. If, in our example company, the gross profit amounts to $2,000,000, then each of 1,000 customers is worth $2,000 in average profitability. If the company's attrition rate is 10 percent, then the cost of attrition is $200,000 ($2,000 x 100). This approach might be useful for high-level planning purposes, but it is useless as a means of understanding the dynamics behind the firm's customer attrition. For one, a supplier who loses high-valued customers—that is, customers of above-average profitability—will be more concerned with *that* fact than with the overall attrition rate or average cost of attrition. For another, this average-costing approach certainly disguises customers who are break-even or being served at a loss.

A fundamental understanding of customer attrition can only be had if the supplier knows *which* customers are defecting, *why* they are defecting, and *how* they might be persuaded to continue to do business with the firm. The analytics necessary to have an in-depth understanding of customer attrition are generally the same as we discussed in chapter 2 while seeking to find the customer's voice for direction in product and service design initiatives: granular segmentation of the customer base, continuous monitoring of satisfaction along those segments, and an understanding of each customer's profitability. The combination of these techniques can prove to be an effective bulwark against defection.

*Customer attrition* in the conventional sense of the term is defined to mean a customer who has *already* defected to a competitor. In most cases, it is true; customers just bolt to a competitor. In my experience, however, many times customers signal their intent to eventually defect by exhibiting a decrementing pattern of spending. This process of *gradual attrition,* if detected sufficiently early, gives the supplier time to respond. Understanding the customer's motivation behind the new pattern of spending provides the supplier an opportunity to stem the tide with newly launched service initiatives, for the benefit of high-valued customers, or to simply ignore the impending defection for customers of marginal value.

An additional consideration in coming to terms with the cost of attrition involves viewing the cost of new customer acquisitions as, *in fact,* a cost of attrition. In our example above, there is every reason to believe that the marketing and sales budget was set at $1,000,000 because of the attrition experienced by the firm. We can ask the question this way: would the company have the same marketing spend if its customer attrition rate were significantly lower? It isn't likely. In the case where new customer acquisitions equal roughly the loss of existing customers, it can be said that the entire marketing and sales budget of $1,000,000 is an additional cost of customer attrition. In other words, the whole marketing and sales budget has gone to simply *replace* lost customers.

Any material reduction in attrition gives executive leadership a number of options that it might not otherwise have. One option available in the light of a lower attrition rate might be to simply reduce the marketing and sales budget—good luck taking that idea to the marketing department!—and take the savings to the bottom line. A smarter option, however, might be to *redirect* some of the marketing and sales budget dollars toward service initiatives—additional frontline personnel, new quality programs, and so forth—all intended to further reduce attrition rate.

As a rule, increasing revenues from existing customers drops the amount that the marketing organization must spend to generate the same amount of revenues from new customers. In some cases, the reduction in cost can be dramatic. If an existing customer can yield in additional revenues and margins what an average new customer generates, then practically the entire marketing cost of finding the next customer can be offset by the supplier. Other benefits accrue to a smart customer retention strategy. First, the longer a supplier commands a customer relationship, the more profitable the customer's business becomes. This is so, because, over time, as customer and supplier organizations learn to work with each other, operating and administrative efficiencies take hold, thereby increasing supplier margins. Second, existing customers, as the source of new business referrals, also mitigate the cost to the supplier of finding the next customer. In addition, a new customer arrived at via a referral has not only the effect of further solidifying the supplier's relationship with the existing customer, but also getting the new relationship off on more solid footing. Finally, a customer of long tenure is more value driven—that is, it is less price sensitive—and thus gives the supplier the flexibility to operate within a broader range of pricing options.

Customer retention strategies are, at bottom, service strategies. And, despite all that these strategies have to recommend them, they are hardly in the marketing mainstream. Yet it is a sobering thought to consider that a supplier will not experience sustainable growth until such time as it becomes as adept at retaining existing customers as it is at attracting new ones.

## DON'T FIRE THAT CUSTOMER—YET!

As we said in chapter 2, it is prudent to segment the customer set on the basis of profitability as well as other dimensions in order to design intelligent marketing strategies that can resonate with individual customers. One of the consequences of this segmentation might be to fire customers who aren't carrying their own weight. You've heard the oft-cited shibboleth that if we fire such and such a customer, we'll make more money. The assumption in these cases is that a customer doesn't throw off enough margin to cover the cost of servicing. That may be true, but the devil of such an action is in the details. My preference is not to automatically fire a customer on the basis of subpar margin outcomes. A preferred approach is to first try to turn the unprofitable customer into a profitable one. This can only be done if the supplier has appropriately segmented the customer base, so as to understand not only the individual customer's profitability but also the customer's spending patterns of behavior in the light of our marketing efforts. If we haven't marketed a consumer loan to a customer, there is a very good chance he will not have purchased one from us! An intelligent approach to upsell an unprofitable customer with additional goods and services should always be the precursor to attrition motivated by the supplier.

Consider the following example from the real world. During a two-year stretch, we serviced a customer whose profitability was break-even at the gross-margin level. The calls from some of our executives to fire the customer were frequent, and they were loud. These executives had a point. Some of us, however, came to a different conclusion. This customer had great equity potential. The customer was a multibillion-dollar division of an international plumbing and heating distributor, which had proved especially difficult to penetrate at the management level. Our strategy was clear: to serve this customer to the best of our ability while continuing to market them hard for additional business. After two years, we were rewarded with a three-year multimillion-dollar deal!

Our construct of the service ethic makes clear that the quality of service must be uniform across the entire customer set at all times. This needs to be the rule until such time as the decision has been made to fire the customer. Furthermore, purposeful service degradation—ignoring the customer's service calls; failing to inform the customer of new products, tools, and services; and so forth—cannot be used as an implement to drive away the marginally profitable customer. Those actions are ethically indefensible. In any event, the decision to fire a customer—clearly a prerogative of the enterprise—should be thoroughly well thought out.

## POOR SERVICE PLACES A HEAVY TAX ON BUSINESS

Economists agree that the first principle of economics is scarcity. In our context, that means customers: precious commodities, expensive to acquire, and in hot demand by the competition. These same precious commodities, however, are all too easily squandered through poor service practices. Here is a hypothetical example from the banking industry: In the United States, there are approximately 3,700 commercial banks with assets between $100 million and $1 billion. Each of these banks has, on average, roughly 200,000 retail depositors—time, demand, and savings depositors. If one applies an industry standard customer attrition rate of 10 percent, then, on average, each bank has to replace approximately 20,000 customers each year (the only caveat in this data is that the use of averages disguises the far smaller depositor base of the smaller asset banks). If we could wave a wand and magically halve the industry standard attrition rate, each bank would still have to replace 10,000 customers annually!

Now, does this sound like we treat customers as precious commodities? Here is a real example based on our work with a customer. A hotel executive in Las Vegas bemoaned that at his particular property, 12 to 15 guests a week check out early after frustrated attempts to camp on the hotel's wireless hotspot. The impact on the hotel's finances are immediately obvious: the forfeiture of the guests' wireless access fees as well as the loss of occupancy at each guest's stipulated hotel room rate. The impact, however, is potentially more profound: these guests and their colleagues, with whom this story will inevitably be shared, will not stay at this particular hotel again until such time as they are assured wireless access has been restored and is functioning smoothly.

In a very real way, poor service saddles a business with a tax that makes anything a governmental body might levy seem like kids' play. Poor service has the same effect on the business as a tax has: it creates economic inefficiencies for the enterprise and distorts a clear picture of the firm's operating cost structure and thus its ability to price its goods and services properly. As with any tax structure, the higher the tax rate the less money we have to spend. Is a 10 percent attrition rate a cost of doing business? What about 8 percent? Each of these attrition assumptions impacts the supplier's bottom line differently.

As we noted in the previous section, a reduction in customer attrition can translate into significant cost reductions for the supplier. All things being equal, a supplier with a lower attrition rate clearly has the added flexibility of operating at a lower cost posture. As we noted, the money can be channeled into new service initiatives— always my stated bias—it can be used to more aggressively price the product or service, or it can be returned to stockholders among other options.

The analogy of poor service to taxes, however, is not a perfect one: taxes are involuntary payments and clearly outside of our control. Customer attrition, on the other hand, is clearly within the control of the enterprise and is not inherently a cost of doing business unless the enterprise chooses to ignore its ability to formulate strategies designed to retain customers.

## PURCHASING AS A COMPETITIVE SPORT

No organization, no matter how capable, can afford to be self-sufficient in the service and information age. The opportunities and the technologies are too numerous and quick to change. Intellectual capital, the principal fuel for growth in the new economy, is too diverse and distributed far beyond the firm's borders. Information, too, is diffused and largely distributed outside the organization. It is sensible, then, that the enterprise seeks out suppliers that can work with them in partnership. In the service and information age, supplier partners can be a force multiplier with the potential to extend the reach of even the mightiest corporation

Unfortunately, the prevalent model in business-to-business relationships today remains an outdated *procurement,* or *purchasing,* model. This model is largely administrative and clerical, having more to do with the mechanics of bid solicitations and contract negotiations than with strategic relationship management. This approach to purchasing is a remnant of the industrial-age fixation with short-term financial results. A large portion—in some cases as much as 60–80 percent—of a company's cost of sales are purchased costs, and so, on the face of it, it seems eminently logical that the procurement focus should rest almost entirely on achieving transactional cost economies. This view of the customer-supplier relationship, however, is counterproductive.

A purchasing practice that entails extracting the best possible price from a supplier and using that as leverage to strike an even better price deal with another supplier will sour any attempt at building a strategic supplier relationship. Purchasing professionals fail to realize that suppliers have figured out this two-step. Suppliers chosen on the basis of price alone return the favor by never straying one iota from a stipulated contract provision that might eat into expected margins. These suppliers, justifiably, turn their focus away from serving the customer to cutting corners to defend their own economies.

Lots of relationships, all of them a mile wide and an inch deep, fall far short of serving the customer as effectively as a few relationships with chosen strategic partners.

These days, a trend is slowly but surely emerging. The customer selects a few, rather than many, suppliers and gets into tightly coupled relationships for the satisfaction of many of its needs. The selection criteria for choice of a strategic partner include not only the supplier's technical qualifications necessary to do the job but also the supplier's culture of service. Compatible cultures are important because the successful strategic relationship relies on there being fundamental trust and confidence among the participants to ensure that nothing is held back in the attainment of common business goals. The result is a relationship where the customer concentrates most of her purchasing dollars on a few key suppliers, in return for suppliers who concentrate their organization's attention, energies, and resources on the customer. The upshot of this type of relationship is a lasting alliance, a long-term relationship that yields benefits unmatched by a strict reliance on transactional cost economies. The short-term financial advantage of doing business along the lines prescribed by the purchasing model of old can never undercut the long-term advantages of improved cost, quality, flexibility, innovation, and service that a customer can derive from a strategic, single-source relationship. But as I said, this will take time to firmly take hold.

## AUCTIONS IN REVERSE

An industrial-age procurement practice dressed in information-age clothing is troubling and deserves a watchful eye. This is the practice of conducting reverse auctions. A reverse auction has the buyer describe the product or service in question to a number of prescreened bidders who on an appointed day submit their bids electronically. The auction software keeps tabs on all bid submissions and assigns each bidder a numeric rank that only that bidder can see. The auction runs for a set period of time, say 30 minutes, with overtime extensions if the top bidders change ranks in the last minutes of the auction. The idea, of course, is to create a bidding frenzy until only one bidder is left standing. The buyer presumably is the beneficiary of the competitive slugfest that ensues and that would not be possible if bids were sealed when submitted. Also, incumbent pricing now becomes easy to validate: the buyer simply conducts an electronic auction periodically or before the current provider's contract is set to expire. If the incumbent's pricing does not win the auction, they will be under intense pressure to match the winning bid. Our company once participated in a reverse auction for a national retailer of office products winning 14 out of 14 bid contests only to learn the incumbent had been left in place. We never had a chance to present and defend our proposal!

The principal benefit to the buyer of entering into a strategic supplier relationship—long-term collaborative problem solving and innovation—is nullified by a reverse auction where nothing but the winning price rules the game. The supplier's reputation, commitment, quality practices, and service principles all are rendered meaningless in a reverse auction process. Suppliers wise to reverse auctions, understandably, strip away every service component not specifically sought by the buyer and lie in wait for any opportunity at retaliatory pricing through change orders. Professor M. L. Emiliani, who has done more work in this area than anyone I have read, suggests that reverse auctions should be recognized for what they are: "A technologically assisted form of power-based bargaining whose benefits for buyers are grossly overstated and which in the long run compromise the mostly shared interests of both buyers and sellers."[7]

## OUTSOURCING: IMPROVED SERVICE OR ECONOMY?

In the early 1980s, Jamaica and Barbados were havens for American companies seeking low-cost data capture services. My company was among those who would fly source documents to these locations and have the encoded and verified data returned as punched cards or diskettes a day or two later. The initial impetus to move these functions offshore had always been the cost advantages offered by these low-wage locations. But we also found a service advantage in outsourcing these functions.

Along the way, we conducted several studies to confirm the principal service advantages of sending these functions offshore: (1) the turnaround time from source document preparation to system input and (2) the accuracy of the transcribed source document data. Time and again, we proved that flying the source documents to one of the islands and returning with the encoded media was more efficient than having these functions performed stateside.

In the 1990s, our company set up software development and maintenance centers offshore from the United States mainland in places like Monterrey, Mexico; Limerick, Ireland; and Bangalore, India. Again, our experience was that customers enjoyed the twin advantages of improved service and cost. In truth, we might have been less aggressive in the pursuit of offshore software development if there had been sufficient numbers of available domestic talent. The reality was that we couldn't find candidates in sufficient numbers that not only mastered a relevant technical discipline but were also proficient in reading, writing, and arithmetic. (When the University of Pennsylvania asked me to address a number of local-area educators about what I thought were the most important qualifications I was looking for in recent graduates, they were chagrined to learn that I stressed the three Rs. "I thought you were a 'computer guy'" was some of the feedback that I received after my talk.)

Senator John Warner of Virginia, chairman of the Armed Services Committee, called the shortage of computer professionals in the late 1990s a "national security issue."[8] The high-tech, foreign guest worker H1B visa program that was supposed to have filled in the gaps for in-country talent shortages was filibustered for so long by opponents, including most notably Senator Tom Harkin of Iowa— the senator did not believe there was a high-tech worker shortage— that, it too, failed to provide the number of workers when it did become a reality. Senator Spencer Abraham of Michigan offered the most prophetic assessment of the situation at the time: "If American companies can't bring the talent here to fill their needs . . . they'll move some of their operations overseas."[9]

In a free market, political hysteria by the anti-outsourcing crowd has to take a back seat to the realities of supply and demand. The consequence of ignoring that rather fundamental rule of economics by clamoring for protectionist policies is to drive wages and living standards *down* not up. Service, however, is as much a consumer staple as are low prices and thus must be balanced by the supplier. Even Wal-Mart, the juggernaut of low-price merchandising in the United States, offers an acceptable—not great by any measure—level of customer satisfaction.

Now comes the outsourcing of manufacturing production to the Far East of products destined not for Asian markets but for North American markets. The infatuation with China, in particular, is now in full swing. U.S.-based original equipment manufacturers (OEMs), apparently bedazzled by the region's low labor rates, are in a pell-mell rush to establish contract manufacturing centers in the Far East. Approximately 50 percent of a worldwide market of nearly $200 billion for electronic manufacturing is based in the region, with the Chinese dragon accounting for approximately 75 percent of the Asian market.

China's cost advantage, however, has begun to slip. India, Thailand, and Vietnam can now offer labor rates below those found in China. The overheated China market has made itself felt in wage inflation of roughly 10 percent per year in technical and professional jobs. This wage inflation has now led to an increased level of job hopping and therefore worker turnover never before seen in China. There is also emerging a serious shortage of skilled manufacturing, quality control, and middle-management workers, precisely the kind of workers sought by OEMs. Further diminishing the allure of China as a manufacturing destination is the steady appreciation of the Chinese currency—the renminbi or RMB—against the U.S. dollar. In any event, Chinese manufacturers—or those located in other Far East destinations—will, for some time to come, enjoy a labor cost advantage vis-à-vis their North American manufacturing counterparts.

If the expected labor cost advantages of sending production offshore are clear, what about the service advantages? A 7,000-mile, multimode journey to the United States from the Far East takes time—lots of time. In a recent survey, approximately 50 percent of respondents suggested that manufacturing orders sourced in China took more than 60 days to be received stateside. Never mind that crude oil bounces around $100 a barrel. Today, the cost of having product stuck in a supply chain for weeks, if not months, has as much to do with the fact that the product has to pass through so many hands—manufacturers, forwarders, customs officials, regulators, shippers, ports, inspectors, and so forth—as with the actual cost of transportation.

The long cycle time inherent in offshore production to the Far East has more insidious consequences that will not only drive total costs up but drive service down. These surround the OEMs inability to forecast the right quantities of product to deal with the vicissitudes of a labyrinthine supply line. Is it reasonable, to assume that a forecast can accurately lock in demand months in advance? How does the OEM provide service and warranty in the United States for product manufactured overseas? How does the supply chain respond to unexpected changes in demand? I know an OEM that sources parts from the Far East for the assembly of a computer appliance in the United States. The CEO of this company has told me that he cannot keep a smooth and uninterrupted supply of parts coming in from the Far East to adequately feed his production line. His customer has told him that they are concerned about the erratic nature of shipments. In response, the OEM has had to borrow heavily from the bank in order to finance a steady supply of product for his customer. At last count, the company was in negotiations to sell itself to a larger competitor as it could no longer sustain the cost of financing. As other companies have found, this OEM learned the hard way that total logistics costs can nullify the advantage of cheap Far East labor.

China has long operated a top-down, command economy—despite the country's rhetoric to embrace free-market mechanisms. One does business in China against a backdrop of opaque rules and regulations. Many of these rules transcend the official judicial framework and are clearly biased to protect the home country. The new China is not much changed in this regard.

Twenty years ago, our company received a delegation of computer technicians—including a designated apparatchik in full Mao regalia—from the People's Republic of China. The delegation was in the United States, courtesy of the United Nations, visiting various computer service companies to learn about new methods of plant automation. The meeting was friendly but tense. The Chinese wanted to automate a huge steel complex employing tens of thousands of workers using mostly manual methods of record keeping. Time and again, the lead spokesman for the delegation would ask me to tell him what size computers were best suited for his steel mill application. I would respond that without far more additional information than he was sharing, I couldn't be of much help. No matter. The same question was repeated several times. I had an interpreter on our side, and so I knew that our failure to communicate was not a linguistic failure. In the end, the Chinese never volunteered any additional information. I believe to this day that the delegation left our meeting believing we knew the answer to their question. I also believe that it was their attitude of mistrust, their xenophobia even, that impeded a frank exchange that might have allowed us to help them.

Of further concern to the West should be that more and more non-market solutions will be sought by China to deal with everything from national insecurities to energy and commodity shortages. Clearly, these issues are more ominous than having to communicate with a source of supply 12 time zones away or having to slog through almost impenetrable language barriers.

The sourcing of product along the Silk Road has made for a complicated, risky, and unpredictable supply chain for thousands of years. To be sure, OEMs have a responsibility to their shareholders *and* customers to explore the most cost-effective way to make product. Just as important, however, OEMs must balance service to the customer with manufacturing economies. No customer I know will trade lousy service for low cost. In light of what we know today, however, it's clear that the service inefficiencies and business risks of outsourcing production to the Far East have begun to trump the advantage of cheap manufacturing labor.[10]

### WHAT'S SERVICE GOT TO DO WITH IT?

In the same way that the United States has ceded vast swaths of its manufacturing sectors to overseas producers, so too, are we in danger of losing much of our service industry. It might be comforting to chuckle at the singsong speech of the young man or woman call-center attendant in Manila, the Philippines, who is trying to help a U.S. caller identify an unauthorized charge on his telephone bill (never mind that the attendant is most likely fluent in two other languages besides English!). Rest assured, however, that the Filipinos, the Indians, the Malaysians, and others will eventually overcome their accentuation and inflection difficulties with the English language, and when next we call to ask about a questionable charge on our phone bill we won't know if the attendant is in Manila or in Omaha. We will chuckle no more.

In a similar vein, I am reminded that when I was in graduate school—admittedly a very long time ago—it was widely believed that software engineering would never slip from our grasp as manufacturing was then just beginning to do in a big way. The conventional wisdom, so it ran, was that the Asians—meaning the East Asians generally, and the Chinese specifically—could not master the intricacies of computer programming. The implication was that Asian cognition was somehow different: it was holistic, contextual, intuitive, and tolerant of ambiguity. In contrast, computer programming as a hierarchical, procedural, precise, and sequential process seemed to be tailor made for the more analytical Western mind. Surprise, surprise. The Chinese have apparently shed their cognitive baggage! The Chinese are not quite there yet, but in another 10 years, perhaps, they will be in a position to challenge the Indians for dominance in software engineering on the world stage.

It should be noted that the threat to our service industries isn't confined to the Far East. In addition to the threats posed by the current front runners in Eastern Europe—Czech Republic, Hungary, Poland, and Russia—I have personally met with delegations from two other countries you might not think are in the same league: Egypt and Morocco. Each has the potential to play the role of spoiler on the world stage. Both countries, besides offering the obvious wage-cost benefits, provide tax-free zones, efficient broadband communication access, and a highly educated and multilingual workforce. There is more. This workforce, as many employers who have taken their business offshore can attest, is very grateful to have jobs and will reward the employer with little absenteeism or turnover.

If all of this isn't enough to cast a pall over the future of much of our service industries, consider a recent trend: American firms outsourcing Spanish-language call-center services—not just the long-outsourced high-end information technology and business processing services—to locations in South America, notably Argentina, to deal with U.S.-based Hispanic consumers. Think about it. The United States, a nation of roughly 40–50 million Hispanics, is outsourcing its call-center work to Argentina to avail itself of Spanish-language service workers! (In another reminder of the fixation of today's enterprise with short-term results—or perhaps a reflection of the short-term *memories* of enterprise leadership—consider that Argentina has been an economic basket case during the last 30 years, bearing witness to spasms of hyperinflation, civil turmoil, and, most relevant to the foreign investor, defaulting on its debt on four different occasions!)

Is there a lesson in all of this? Recall our discussion in chapter 1 about the likelihood that the modern enterprise, regardless of industry, will be suffused with all manner of service activities and interactions. If manufacturing slipped away from the United States in a generation, it won't take nearly as long for service activities—more easily outsourceable than manufacturing ever was—to disappear from our shores. The process, unfortunately, is already well on its way in fields as diverse as software engineering, product design, call centers, and a number of back-office business processes. If the United States is to avoid a nuclear winter in its service industries, it has no choice but to *excel* in service, do so at *globally competitive* prices, and do so *now*.

# *Epilogue*

I believe I have stated throughout this book why the lens through which participants rooted in the industrial age look at the enterprise is obsolete in the service and information age. It is logical—logical to me, anyway—in the light of our discussion that one should expect the eventual demise of the industrial-age paradigm of how we conduct business generally and how we serve the customer specifically. The industrial-age paradigm, to review, is focused on short-term financial horizons, enterprise measures of efficiency, customer acquisition in favor of customer retention, mass production, and uniformity.

What I am not prepared to argue, however, is that there is a certain inevitability on which we can count that will finally drop the curtain on the current fixation with industrial-age modes of corporate behavior. In other words, I'm not certain that the future is altogether *industrial-age proof*. In 1989, in their book, *Total Customer Service*, authors William H. Davidow and Bro Uttal wrote of a "customer service crisis building throughout the business world."[1] I'm afraid to say that not much has changed in the intervening 20 years but that service has gotten progressively worse.

Two-time U.S. presidential candidate Steve Forbes was the keynote speaker at the opening of our company's Technology Reengineering Center in Scottsdale, Arizona. In his address, Mr. Forbes repeated his oft-stated view that the nation's leaders are adrift. What with high taxes, uncontrollable government spending, bureaucratic meddling, and corruption, among other afflictions, Mr. Forbes believes it is time for a national reawakening. In a similar vein, I believe our nation's business leaders are adrift without a compass to guide the service actions of their organizations. Reversing this trend will require more than a reawakening. In some organizations, it will take an effort of nightmarish proportions. Here is a case in point. Recall from chapter 3 how Siemens AG was caught running what can only be described as a *bazaar* for corruptible government officials and other third parties over a period of seven years, on a global scale, and to the tune of nearly $2 billion. Like so much water off a duck's back, Peter Loescher, president and CEO, had the cheek to say in the foreword to the company's *Business Conduct Guidelines for 2009* that "it is top performance with the highest *ethics* (italics mine) that has made Siemens strong."[2] Mr. Loescher is either spectacularly naïve—not very likely—or he assumes his employees to be, which is far more likely.

If the critical success factors required of the enterprise—*customer-focused leadership, customer-centric strategic planning, an organizational ethic of service,* and *a top-notch front line*—come together only in broad or faint outline, marginal progress may be the end result.

The implementation of the critical success factors, particularly in large and established organizations, will require tough slogging and consume lots of time. Furthermore, there is no cookbook or template formula approach to the implementation of the success factors. This is because so much of the transformational work that must be accomplished is a function of the situational conditions that exist in an organization at a particular point in time.

A genuine attempt at transformation must begin with a disciplined, honest diagnostic—I resist using the word *audit,* but in many ways, that is just what it is—to measure the extent of the gap between the organization's existing mode of operation and the principles and practices of the customer-focused provider. This diagnostic can begin with a well-designed, pretested, and properly administered survey instrument that asks employees to rate their level of agreement, using the five-point Likert scale mentioned in the previous chapter, on enterprise-wide dimensions emblematic of a strong customer focus as well as on dimensions more germane to the local survey population. Free-form comments should also be invited to add color to the forced-choice responses. The first set of dimensions can be assessed by asking respondents to react to statements that have been carefully framed to touch on each of the critical success factors. Specific questions or phrasing, of course, can be nuanced for the employee population being surveyed. Here is a sampling of the questions I would include in a customer-focus diagnostic:

1. The primary mission of this company is that "customers are first."

2. I believe in the mission of this company.
3. My management believes in the mission of this company.
4. The company's code of ethics accurately reflects the organization's values and principles.
5. My management actively seeks my opinion in how best to serve the customer.
6. I bring forward suggestions for service improvement.
7. My management gives me the latitude to do what is right for the customer.
8. The work I do can be traced directly to serving the customer.
9. This company delivers on its promises to customers.
10. I have the information and the tools at my disposal to provide excellence in service to our customers.
11. I am rewarded for providing excellent service to customers.
12. I am knowledgeable of the company's products, services, and processes for which I have responsibility.
13. I receive frequent training on the company's new products, services, and processes.

The list of questions can go on, although the survey should be kept reasonably concise. The second set of dimensions should be tailored for the local employee population and might include questions having to do with the physical condition of the plant, store, or office; staffing levels; working hours; crime in the local area; or any other factor with the potential to affect the manner in which the company serves the customer.

A diagnostic such as this should not be considered, much less launched, unless executive leadership is organized to receive and efficiently process the survey feedback. The first time we conducted an employee survey along the lines outlined above on a company-wide basis, we were overwhelmed by the scale and depth of responses. We simply were not prepared for the onslaught. In retrospect, we could have done a far better job in organizing ourselves to process responses before pulling the trigger on the survey. Most importantly, the leadership needs to be seriously committed to carefully evaluating the survey feedback and acting on ideas of merit. More damage is apt to be caused by launching the diagnostic and then either dismissing its findings out of hand or letting opportunities for improvement languish.

An action plan to address the issues identified in the diagnostic will need to follow a lot of analysis, discussion, and even negotiation to properly rank order—or ultimately dismiss—opportunities for service improvement. For example, a strong disagreement by respondents with the assertion made in question 10 above will potentially entail a lot of research and follow-up to unearth the kinds of "information and tools" sought by the front line to better serve the customer.

A plan of communication to all those affected should precede the implementation phase of substantive remediation actions. The reality is that all but the most simple and straightforward opportunities for improvement might ultimately be dependent on budget availability, hiring decisions, process modifications, system acquisitions, reorganizations, and so on. All of this will take time to plan and execute, and so a final step in the process is the publication of frequent status updates to inform the organization of its transformational efforts. This feedback process, properly administered, has the potential to lift employee morale and job performance. It will also confirm for employees that their voices are indeed being heard. In the end, however, it is the customer that will stand as the key beneficiary of such a transformational process.

This four-step process of *diagnose, plan, implement*, and *review* will have to be revisited with the passage of time or triggered in response to material changes in corporate structure—perhaps the result of mergers, acquisitions, or dispositions—to ensure the organization's needle is always pointing toward a customer focus. Also, it is clear that this process militates against quick results and thus might compel organizations to abort the process anywhere along its arduous journey. At these critical junctures, it will take strong executive leadership to provide any necessary course corrections. Other issues loom large as well.

If we have been traveling through time toward ever-increasing levels of awareness that service is central to the business of the enterprise—arguable on many levels as I've pointed out in this book—I believe that the progress that's been made could become retrograde at any point. A corporate financial emergency, a management shake-up, discontent by an institutional investor (seeking improved results *this* quarter), a deep recession, a terrorist act, or dramatic political shifts in the country all have the potential to snap us back to where we again become more comfortable with the old and familiar smokestack mentality—with efficiency as the rallying cry—of how we should run a business. The subprime mortgage crisis about which we have spoken in this book is a case in point.

Whatever the attribution of this crisis is assumed to be—the monetary policies of the Federal Reserve, the failure of regulators, arcane accounting rules, greedy businessmen, naïve consumers, mishaps of credit-rating agencies, and so forth—it is, in the end, a failure to *serve*. This is an example of the kind of catatonic event that I fear will reverse whatever progress we've made in serving the consuming public. Consider, for example, that many financial services will be concentrated in a few megabanks: Bank of America, JP Morgan, and Wells Fargo combined will control over 30 percent of the nation's commercial bank deposits! Free from competitive pressures, this cartel will control prices and commoditize service. That's the bad news.

Here's the good news. The days when industrial-age mass marketers told us what to buy are drawing to a close. Today, few customers buy without comparing competitive product and service offerings; fewer still buy on name alone, no matter how exalted the brand. Prospective customers can now tap the Internet and compare product and service features, talk to other customers via on-line chat rooms, read research reports, check out social-networking sites, and study customer survey data on product review sites. In the service and information age, specious supplier claims will have very short half-lives indeed. I found, for instance, that a negative review to Amazon, of one of its downstream suppliers, drew an instant response where repeated direct queries failed to elicit any satisfaction for an improper shipment of merchandise by the supplier. The specter of a negative review in full view of thousands, if not millions, of consumers allows the consumer to level the playing field with careless or irresponsible merchants. The upshot of all of this is that brand distinctions will blur in the absence of meaningful service differences. Further, consumers more than ever before will focus on the integrity of their suppliers as well as on the supplier's products and services.

In a world of skeptical, demanding customers on the one hand and meaningless brand distinctions on the other, a customer-focused supplier can be armed with an unassailable competitive weapon: *excellence in service*. Customer-focused strategies as we have described in this book allow a supplier to establish a rock-solid foundation on which to position its brand where it matters most to customers: in terms of quality and service. And, it allows the supplier to position its brand with sincerity and conviction; attributes that can't be duplicated simply through fancy packaging, dancing monkeys, or advertising pizzazz. In terms that every executive responsible for protecting the integrity of their brand can understand, customer-focused strategies imbue the personality of the brand with characteristics, and values, that can nullify the marketing rhetoric of even the most ably financed competitor in a given market. Reliability, responsiveness, service, and integrity, the stuff of the customer-focused supplier, are values that customers as consumers, as humans, seek to find in their supplier partners and their brands. Even in the newly coagulated financial services marketplace, opportunities will abound for new entrants dedicated to a customer focus.

The dynamics of the service-and-information economy are driving all suppliers to increase the service component of their offerings. Pure service companies will need to expand their range of services outside their traditional sweet spot to remain competitive. Others will have to enhance their competitive offerings by improving the informational content and convenience of their services. Product companies, too, whether they make computer hardware, automobiles, or steel, will see the service component that surrounds their product offerings rise dramatically. The upshot for product companies is that as they experience the steady commoditization of their hard goods, they'll have little choice but to grow increasingly reliant on services if they are to survive, let alone grow, in the new century. An example of this trend comes from our experience with one of our customers who, after a long deliberation, selected a computer maker whose product performance, ergonomic design, and aesthetics were inferior to a competing device—of roughly equal price—to be its strategic computer provider. What was the principal advantage of the winning provider? A superior service and repair warranty offering.

Notwithstanding this apparently madcap chase for opportunities outside a provider's legacy stronghold, suppliers will have to remain price competitive. In other words, improved or enhanced service will offer little or no sanctuary to the high-cost provider. Welcome to the service and information age!

In tandem with this inexorable trend slicing through the economy, and perhaps as a consequence of it, the balance of power in commerce has begun to tip decidedly in favor of the customer. With this newfound clout, customers are beginning to assert themselves and demand undivided and individualized attention to their needs. This devolution of power, from supplier to customer, is leading to a larger, more prominent role for customers in dealing with suppliers.

In health care, the nation's drift toward collectivist medical care—a system where the needs of the individual are subordinated to the needs of the group—will further degrade service in an industry that historically has been characterized by the stifling dominance of its key suppliers: hospitals, clinics, and physicians. Fortunately, the dynamics of the service and information age are certain to level the playing field. Health care portals such as *Web*Md, The Life Extension Foundation, self-help services such as Dr. Russell Blaylock's Wellness Report, and new health care delivery mechanisms will allow consumers to begin to right the imbalance back in their favor.

The rise of retainer medical care—physician practices that choose to serve a small number of patients in return for a yearly retainer fee—is a case in point. Retainer medicine is now a well-established and growing niche in health care, clearly serving a need in the marketplace that has not been met by third-party health plans. The results of retainer medical care have been impressive: hospitalization rates 80 percent lower for retainer medicine patients than for patients of conventional health plans; increased access, day or night, to physician care and consultation; and improved patient satisfaction as evidenced by a renewal rate in excess of 90 percent for retainer services. I switched to retainer medicine after years of getting nothing more than recorded messages whenever I called my doctor to ask a question or to schedule an appointment. (When my wife asked the doctor to have an MRI done of her rotator cuff, which was causing her much pain, the doctor, not entirely tongue-in-cheek, said, "Mrs. Pupo, what would you have done before the advent of the MRI?") I now have a physician who answers his cell phone after-hours, makes house calls if I'm too ill to drive to his office, and is proactive in the use of all the tools at his disposal to better treat his patients.

The wonderful thing about this new state of affairs is that it plays to the strengths of the customer-focused supplier. This new breed of supplier is quite comfortable having a collaborative, cooperative relationship with the customer. The customer-focused supplier is not only willing but also adept at sharing vital information with its customers—asking questions, seeking feedback, learning, and trusting.

I have found the principles and practices described in this book to be highly effective in sustaining satisfied, loyal, and, ultimately, more profitable customers. But there is much more. These practices require that the supplier organization behaves ethically and morally, both inside and outside the supplier's walls. The practices of the customer-focused supplier simply cannot thrive in a corporate environment of institutionalized mistrust, of individual self-interest, devoid of courage, character, and integrity. It simply will not survive these corrosive elements.

Customer-focused strategies are a powerful and motivating reward for the customer-focused organization's customers, employees, and leadership. They help build morale and create an environment where people are reassured and supported in doing the right thing. The customer-focused provider manages to set itself free from the tyranny of industrial-age priorities by balancing a higher moral and aesthetic purpose with the need to remain financially viable. Suppliers who can harmonize these often competing dimensions through the principles and practices espoused in this book will have a decided edge in the 21st century.

# Notes

## PREFACE

1. Humberto E. Fontova, *Fidel: Hollywood's Favorite Tyrant* (Washington, DC: Regnery Publishing, 2005), p. 37.
2. Miguel A. Faria, Jr., *Cuba in Revolution* (Macon, GA: Hacienda Publishing, 2002), pp. 184–223.
3. Mark Reutter, "America's Best-Paid Executive," Making Steel.com, June 1990, p. 2.

## INTRODUCTION

1. *Customer Service Quality Falling Short of Rising Expectations across the Globe,* Accenture Study, January 7, 2008.
2. *Healthcare Consumer Survey,* Katzenbach Partners LLC, 2007.
3. Michael E. Porter, *Competitive Strategy* (New York: The Free Press, 1980).
4. Peter Drucker, *The Post Capitalist Society* (New York: Harper Business, 1993), pp. 6–65.

## CHAPTER 1

1. Len Schlesinger and Bill Fromm, *The Real Heroes of Business, And Not a CEO among Them* (New York: Currency Doubleday, 1993), p. xx.
2. Susan E. Squires, Cynthia J. Smith, Loma McDougall, and William R. Yeack, *Inside Arthur Andersen: Shifting Values, Unexpected Consequences* (Englewood Cliffs, NJ: Financial Times Prentice Hall, 2003), pp. 96–102.
3. Frederick Reichheld, *The Loyalty Effect* (Boston, MA: Harvard School Press, 1996), p. 309.
4. Niccolò Machiavelli, *The Prince*, trans. W. K. Marriott and Dominic Baker-Smith (New York: Everyman's Library, 1992), p. 25.

5. Ibid.

6. "Customer Orientation Survey," Walker Information, November 1998.

7. Jim Clawson, *Organizational Charters: Mission, Vision, Values, Strategies and Goals* (Charlottesville: University of Virginia Darden School Foundation, 1996).

8. "Toyota Denied Sudden Acceleration Problem for More Than 5 Years," InjuryBoard.com, November 6, 2009, http://kansascity.injuryboard.com/automobile-accidents/toyota-denied-customer-complaints-on-sudden-acceleration-problem-for-more-than-5-years.aspx?googleid=274028.

9. "Toyota 'deliberately withheld' evidence in safety lawsuits House panel says," Los Angeles Times, February 27, 2010, http://articles.latimes.com/2010/feb/27/business/la-fi-toyota-biller28-2010feb28.

10. "Wachovia Ranks No. 1 in Customer Satisfaction Survey for Seventh Straight Year," February 19, 2008, http://wachovia.com/inside/page/0.

11. "Papers Show Wachovia Knew of Thefts," *New York Times*, February 6, 2008, http://www.nytimes.com/2008/02/06/business/06wachovia.html.

12. "Big Fine Set for Wachovia to End Case," *New York Times*, April 26, 2008, http://www.nytimes.com/2008/04/26/business/26banks.html.

13. "Wachovia Settles Auction-Rate Securities Probe," Reuters, August, 15, 2008, http://www.reuters.com/article/idUSN1529836120080815.

14. "Fed Approves Wells Fargo's Wachovia Acquisition," Fox News.com, October 12, 2008, http://www.foxnews.com/printer_friendly_story/0,3566,436661,00.html.

15. Lord Acton, *History of Freedom,* (London: Macmillan, 1907).

16. John Kenneth Galbraith, *The Culture of Contentment* (Boston, MA: Houghton Mifflin Company, 1992), p. 69.

17. "Wachovia Bank, N.A. Settles Previously Disclosed Compílanse Matters," Business Wire, March 17, 2010, http://www.marketwatch.com/story/wachovia-bank-na-settles-previously-disclosed-compliance-matters.

18. Karl Albrecht and Ron Zemke, *Service America!* (New York: Warner Books, 1985), p. 106.

19. *Hospital Check-Up Report: Nurse and Employee,* Press Ganey Associates, 2007.

20. Max Weber, *The Theory of Social and Economic Organization*, trans. and ed. A.M. Henderson, and Talcott Parsons (New York: Oxford University Press, 1947).

21. Jan Carlzon, *Moments of Truth,* (New York: Harper Collins, 1987), p. 3.

22. "An Ocean Apart," Storefront Backtalk, June 27, 2008, http://www.storefrontbacktalk.com/category/e-commerce/page/8/.

23. Lorraine Spurge, *Failure Is Not an Option: How MCI Invented Competition in Telecommunications* (Encino, CA: Spurge Ink! 1998), p. 258.

24. Ibid., pp. 5–6.

25. Ibid., p. 31.


## CHAPTER 2

1. John Kenneth Galbraith, *The New Industrial State* (Boston, MA: Houghton Mifflin Company, 1967), p. 6.

2. Report of the National Intelligence Council's 2020 Project, December 2004.

3. F. A. Hayek, *Individualism and Economic Order* (Chicago: The University of Chicago Press, 1948), p. 78.

4. Henry Mintzberg, *The Rise and Fall of Strategic Planning* (New York: The Free Press, 1994), p. 5.

5. "Trends I'm Watching: The Erosion of Trust—CPI and GDP Distorted for Political Purposes," http://www.trendsimwatching.com/2009/04/.

6. Mintzberg, *The Rise and Fall of Strategic Planning*, p. 321.

7. George A. Steiner, *Strategic Planning* (New York: The Free Press, 1979), p. 14.

8. Frederick Taylor, *The Principles of Scientific Management* (New York: Harper & Brothers Publishers, 1911), pp. 25–42.

9. Michael Burgan, *Henry Ford* (New York: Gareth Stevens Publishers, 2002), p. 4.

10. Leonard Mlodinow, *Feynman's Rainbow* (New York: Warner Books, 2003), p. xii.

11. Drusilla Scott, *Everyman Revived: The Common Sense of Michael Polanyi* (Grand Rapids, MI: Wm. B. Eerdmans Publishing Company, 1995), p. 48.

12. "You Can't Innovate Like Apple," *The Pragmatic Marketer* 6, no. 4 (2008), p. 8.

13. Winston Churchill quoted in David Chandler, *The Military Maxims of Napoleon* (New York: McMillan Publishing Company, 1987), p. 87.

14. Clayton M. Christensen, *The Innovator's Dilemma: When New Technologies Cause Great Firms to Fail* (Boston, MA: Harvard Business School Press, 1997), p. 178.

15. Seraku N. Kano, N. Takahash, and S. Tsuji, "Attractive Quality and Must Be Quality," *Quality, The Journal of Japanese Society for Quality Control* 14, no. 2 (1984), pp. 39–48.

16. "Prudential Chief Knew about Payment, Lawyer Testified," *New York Times*, December 21, 1997 http://www.nytimes.com/1997/12/21us/prudential-chief-knew-about-payment; "Appeals Court Panel Upholds Prudential Insurance Settlement," *New York Times*, July 24, 1998 http://www.nytimes.com/1998/07/24/business/appeals-court-panel-

upholds-prudential-insurance-settlement; "Pru Agrees to $600 Million Market-Timing Settlement," registeredrep.com, August 29, 2006, http://registered.com/news/Pru_Market-Timing_Settlement/.

17. "Judge Doesn't Sign Off on BofA SEC Settlement," Pro2net.com, August 6, 2009, http://www.pro2net.com/x67327.xml.

18. The Securities and Exchange Commission, "New York Attorney General's Office, NASD and the New York Stock Exchange Permanently Bar Jack Grubman and Require $15 Million Payment," April 28, 2003, http://www.sec.gov/news/press/2003-55.htm.

19. "The 'Good Hands' Company or a Leader in Anti-Consumer Practices?" Consumer Federation of America, July 18, 2007.

20. "Allstate to Cut Rates in Settlement with Florida," NewsDaily. com, August 15, 2008, http://www.newsdaily.com/stories/n15459807-allstate-florida/.

21. Testimony of J. Robert Hunter, Director of Insurance, Consumer Federation of America, Before the Committee on the Judiciary of the U.S. Senate, March 7, 2007.

22. "Qwest Maps Out a New Escape Plan," TELEPHONY ONLINE, April 7, 2003, http://telephonyonline.com/broadband/print/telecom_qwest_maps_new/.

## CHAPTER 3

1. "SEC Charges Siemens AG for Engaging in Worldwide Bribery," LawFuel.com, December 15, 2008, http://www.lawfuel.com/show-release.asp?ID=20222.

2. Ethics Resource Center, National Business Ethics Survey, 2007.

3. Herbert A. Davidson, *Moses Maimonedes, The Man and His Works* (New York: Oxford University Press, 2005), pp. 168–86.

4. Samuel P. Huntington, *The Clash of Civilizations and the Remaking of the World Order* (New York: Simon & Schuster, 1996), p. 59.

5. John Berlau, "A Tremendously Costly Law," *National Review Online,* April 2005, p. 3.

6. R. Preston McAfee, Nicholas V. Vakkur, and Fred Kipperman, "The Real Costs of Sarbanes-Oxley," *LRN-RAND Center Study,* January 14, 2008, p. 15.

7. "SEC Fines GE $50 Million for Accounting Misdeeds," Businessweek.com, August 4, 2009, http://www.businessweek.com/print/bwdaily/dnflash/content/aug2009.

8. Bernard Ascher, "The Audit Industry: World's Weakest Oligopoly," The American Antitrust Institute, August 2008, p. 3.

9. Lowell McAdam, "A Message to All Employees," Verizon Wireless, *Your Code of Conduct*, May 2008.

10. Jeffrey Abrahams, *101 Mission Statements* (Berkeley, CA: Ten Speed Press, 2007).

11. Edwards Deming, *Out of the Crisis* (Cambridge, MA: MIT, 1982), p. 5.

12. L. L. Barry, A. Parasuraman, and V. A. Zeithaml, *Service Quality*, ed. Roland T. Rust and Richard L. Oliver (Thousand Oaks, CA: Sage Publications, 1994), p. 5.

13. "Air Passengers' No. 1 Complaint: Service," *CNN Money*, June 17, 2008, http://cnnmoney.printthis.clickability.com/pt/cpt?action=cpt&title=Study%3A+Airline+cu.

14. Yoji Akao and Shigeru Mizuno, *QFD: Customer Driven Approach* (London: Taylor & Francis, 1994).

15. Don Peppers and Martha Rogers, *The One to One Future* (New York: Currency Doubleday, 1997), pp. 64–67.

16. Chip Bell, *Customers as Partners* (San Francisco, CA: Berrett-Koehler Publishers, 1996), pp. 8–11.

17. Robert C. Solomon, *Ethics and Excellence, Cooperation and Integrity in Business* (New York: Oxford University Press, 1993), p. 38.

18. Rupert Brooke, *The Collected Poems of Rupert Brooke* (London: Sid Gwick & Jackson, 1918), p. 127.

19. "Metropolitan Life in Accord for Settlement of Fraud Suits," *New York Times*, August 19, 1999, http://query.nytimes.com/gst/fullpage.html?9407E2D81738F93AA2575BCOA96F958.

20. Ron Zemke and Kristin Anderson, "Customers from Hell," *Training*, February, 1990, pp. 25–37.

21. Stephen R. Covey, *The 7 Habits of Highly Effective People* (New York: Fireside, 1990), p. 213.

22. James Hillman, *Kinds of Power* (New York: Currency Doubleday, 1995), p. 69.

23. David S. Landes, *The Wealth and Poverty of Nations* (New York: W.W. Norton & Company, 1998), p. 516.

24. "2007 North American Self-Service Kiosks," IHL Consulting Group, July 3, 2007.

25. "Digital Signage—InfoTrends Sees Significant Growth for Narrowcasting," Ezine@rticles, July 5, 2007, http://ezinearticles.com/?Digital-Signage—InfoTrends-Sees-Significant-Growth-for-Narrow casting&id=633856.

## CHAPTER 4

1. Howard E. Gardner, *Frames of Mind: The Theory of Multiple Intelligences* (New York: Basic Books, 1983).

2. 2003 National Assessment of Adult Literacy, U.S. Department of Education.

3. "In a Global Test of Math Skills, U.S. Students Behind the Curve," *Washington Post*, December 7, 2004, http://washingtonpost.com/ac2/wp-dyn/A41278-2004Dec6?language=printer.

4. Robert Merton, *Social Theory and Social Structure* (New York: Free Press, 1968).

5. "Starbucks Stores to Shut 3 Hours on February 26 for Retraining Baristas," *Seattle Times*, February 12, 2008, http://seattletimes.nwsource.com/cgi-bin/PrintStory.pl?document_id=2004177542.

6. "Comair to Replace Old System that Failed," *USA Today*, December 28, 2004, http://usatoday.printthis.clickability.com/pt/cpt?action=cpt&title=USATODAY.com+-+Co.

7. "Purchases Trigger Overdraft Fees Before They Clear," *USA Today*, August 6, 2008, http://www.tripinsurancestore.com/blog/debit-card-purchases-trigger-overdraft-fees-before-they-clear/.

8. R. J. Sternberg, G. B. Forsythe, J. Hedlund, J. A. Horvath, R. K. Wagner, W. M. Williams, S. A. Snook, and E. L. Grigorenko, *Practical Intelligence in Everyday Life* (Cambridge, UK: Cambridge University Press, 2000).

## CHAPTER 5

1. Stephen Birmingham, *Our Crowd* (Syracuse, NY: Syracuse University Press, 1967), pp. 34–35.

2. Ibid., p. 37.

3. "Customer Satisfaction and Stock Prices: High Returns, Low Risk," *Journal of Marketing* 70 (January 2006): 3–14.

4. "Banking on Illegal Immigrants," *Los Angeles Times*, February 14, 2007.

5. Frederick F. Reichheld, ed., "The Quest for Loyalty," *Harvard Business Review*, 1996, p. xvi.

6. Yasuyuki Fuchita, "Surveys as a Means of Improving Disclosure," *Nomura Capital Market Review* 8, no. 3 (Autumn 2005): 114–20.

7. M. L. Emiliani and D. J. Stec, "Commentary on the Paper 'Reverse Auctions for Relationship Marketers'," *Industrial Marketing Management* 34 (2005): 170.

8. George Leopold, "U.S. Needs 95,000 New Info Workers per Year," *Electronic Engineering Times*, October 2, 1997.

9. "Senate OK's Bill to Increase High-Tech Worker Visas," *Los Angeles Times*, May 19, 1998.

10. "Why Contract Manufacturing in the U.S. Makes All the Sense in the World," EMSNOW, October 23, 2007, http://www.emsnow.com/cnt/files/White%20Papers/TIS_US_Contract_Mfg.pdf.

## EPILOGUE

1. William H. Davidow and Bro Uttal, *Total Customer Service* (New York: Harper & Row Publishers, 1989), p. 1.

2. Peter Loescher, "Foreword," in *Siemens Business Conduct Guidelines 2009*, January 2009, p. 3.

# Index

# About the Author

RAUL PUPO is an entrepreneur, author, speaker, and consultant in the information technology industry. He has also served as an adjunct professor in management information systems, as a reviewer for the peer-reviewed scholarly journal *MIS Quarterly*, and as a board member advising the information technology institutes of several universities.

Pupo is currently CEO of Technology Infrastructure Solutions Inc. (TIS), http://www.deploytis.com, a leader known for its customer service in network integration to *Fortune* 1000 clients. Prior to TIS, Pupo was founder, president, and CEO of PKS Information Services Inc., an international technology services company with operations in Europe, North America, South America, and the Far East. Prior to PKS, Pupo was founder and president of Genix, a pioneer in computer outsourcing. Both PKS and Genix were acquired by *Fortune* 500 technology companies.

Pupo currently serves on the advisory board of Blackhorn Capital, a boutique advisory firm working in the fields of general and financial strategy to companies in the information technology industry.

Pupo has a BBA in industrial management from the University of Miami and an MBA in information systems from the Rochester Institute of Technology. Pupo has also completed all course work for an MS degree in technology management from the University of Pennsylvania.

Pupo has authored many white papers for practitioners in business, and his articles have been published in various newspapers, magazines, and journals. He has lectured before university students and to industry groups. Pupo has also been interviewed on radio and television in Europe.

Pupo's business experience spans nearly 30 years of founding and operating companies in the field of information technology. In each case, these companies achieved success on the strength of Pupo's service philosophy as they were all modestly capitalized while competing against the giants of the technology world.